The Simple Guide to
Freshwater Aquariums
Second Edition

David E. Boruchowitz

Dedication

To my parents, who gave me the means and the latitude to become an aquarist and who instilled in me a love of learning that, nearly six decades later, still illuminates my life.

The Simple Guide to Freshwater Aquariums, Second Edition
Project Team
Editor: Craig Sernotti
Indexer: Lucie Haskins
Series Design: Stephanie Krautheim
Design Layout: Angela Stanford

TFH Publications, Inc.
President/CEO: Glen S. Axelrod
Executive Vice President: Mark E. Johnson
Publisher: Christopher T. Reggio
Production Manager: Kathy Bontz

TFH Publications, Inc.
One TFH Plaza
Third and Union Avenues
Neptune City, NJ 07753

10 11 12 13 14 3 5 7 9 8 6 4
Printed and bound in China
Library of Congress Cataloging-in-Publication Data
Boruchowitz, David E.
  The simple guide to freshwater aquariums / David E. Boruchowitz. -- 2nd ed.
     p. cm.
  Includes index.
  ISBN 978-0-7938-2122-8 (alk. paper)
  1. Aquariums. 2. Aquarium fishes. I. Title.
  SF457.B57 2008
  639.34--dc22
                    2008011960

The Leader in Responsible Animal Care for Over 50 Years!®
www.tfh.com

Table of Contents

Preface to the Second Edition

No other book I have written has gotten the reader response this one has. Over the years emails continue to arrive from people who read this book, follow it, have a successful experience with a first aquarium, and go on in the hobby. It is extremely gratifying, and I am smart enough to know not to fix what isn't broken. Nevertheless, readers' comments and my own learning and observation have prompted a few tweaks to the book. Thus this edition is updated and formatted to be even more user friendly, but all of the crucial information from the first edition remains, though in some cases it has been clarified. As just one example, the information which I identify as the most important in the book—the information about tank cycling—has been updated to reflect both reader feedback and the progression of knowledge in the hobby.

There is one change that might seem to be significant. In this second edition, I have decided to remove almost all of the little bit of water chemistry I included in the first edition. This does not reflect a change in the advice I give, which is to ignore pH, alkalinity, and hardness issues unless you have an extreme situation with your tap water. It is merely an evolution in my continual attempts to provide new aquarists with a protocol that will ensure their success with their first tank. Many new aquarists needlessly fuss with their water chemistry—to their fish's detriment—but almost no new aquarists have tap water that is unsuitable for fishkeeping. It is therefore in keeping with the goal of this book to eliminate a discussion of material over which a new aquarist does not need to fret. As always, there is plenty of time to learn such material after you are a successful aquarist—if you wish to. There are some species that need very specific water chemistry, especially for breeding, but without exception those are not fish for beginning aquarists. This is probably the most iconoclastic of the ideas you'll find between these covers, and it's sure to raise cries of protests from many. Ignore those protestations. This book is meant to smash icons, and to change the aquarium world, in which two out of every three new members to that world leave it within a year. That is something truly worth changing!

David E. Boruchowitz
Covert, NY
November 2007

Guide to the Guide

A *simple* guide? You might ask yourself how this book can be a simple guide but be more than 250 pages long. Well, everything is relative. A simple guide to separating eggs might need only a sentence or two and a couple of pictures. A simple guide to calculating favorable Earth-Mars trajectories might need several volumes bigger than this book. In writing a simple guide about setting up your first freshwater aquarium, I have to cover a lot of material—far short of all the material that *could* be covered, but still a reasonable amount.

To help make sense of all this material, I've broken the book into separate parts. A major portion of the first section identifies the biggest reasons why many of the people who try fishkeeping give up and, keeping things as simple as possible, specifies the science you need to understand to be successful with your first aquarium and not become part of the give-up group.

Part 2, "Sifting Through the Hardware," does just that. It covers what equipment you actually need, and why. It also talks about what equipment you *don't* need, because if an aquarium is properly planned and set up, the amount of equipment needed is really quite small. Much more important is the *knowledge* needed to have a successful first tank. If you read and follow this book, you'll wind up with a lot of valuable knowledge, but not necessarily a lot of expensive equipment. That is, you won't have a lot of expensive equipment unless you *want* to have a lot of expensive equipment. Which is perfectly okay. That's the way some people enjoy a hobby best—if they can indulge their passion for having the biggest and the best and

A Note on Measurements

When we convert between American System measurements and Metric System measurements, we use rounded-off conversions to provide equivalent levels of precision. Readers familiar with the mathematical concept of significant figures will recognize that these rounded conversions, while less precise, are actually more accurate *because* they are less precise. Where measurements are only approximate to begin with, as in the nominal gallonage of various standard aquarium sizes (where the actual volume is often quite different from the named size), we use only approximate round conversions.

the fanciest and the most up to date and the most all-around geewhizziest. I'm certainly not going to stand in your way if that's your style, because that style of maximizing pleasure from a hobby is as good as any other—I just want to point out that you don't have to spend as much as you might have been led to believe to enjoy the aquarium hobby.

Having covered the equipment needed and the choices involved, we then go on in Part 3 to the actual setting up and maintaining of your tank. By the time you finish this section, you'll know how to select equipment, set it up, and maintain it, and many books stop right there. Well, the most carefully set up and best-running aquarium in the world will fail if the fish chosen for it are inappropriate, so I've included Part 4, "Research and Planning." You see, you're facing a circular problem as a new aquarist—you need experience to make certain judgments sensibly, but if you make the wrong judgments your tank may fail and you'll never get the experience! That's why this section of the book is designed to give you a feel for the important topics that you can master only with experience. You aren't left on your own; I've given you many examples that—if you follow them—will guide you to a successful first aquarium.

The final elements of the book add to this by listing some concise reference material and summaries of some of the knowledge given in the rest of the book.

So that's how this simple guide is put together. My goal in writing it was to provide someone interested in becoming an aquarist with the simplest, most direct way of attaining that goal. For me, it was a labor of love, an attempt to share the joy that tropical fish have brought me throughout my life. I hope that they'll do the same for you.

Part 1: So You Think You Want to Be an Aquarist?

While millions of people enjoy keeping an aquarium, the hobby isn't for everyone. The idea obviously holds some attraction for you, since you're reading this book. Here in Part 1 we'll go over some basic pros and cons, and we'll tell you what you can expect as an aquarist. That way you can make an informed decision about whether to take the first steps to becoming a fishkeeper, which the rest of this book will outline for you.

Chapter 1

A Natural Choice

Keeping an aquarium is one way of bringing a bit of nature into your home. Every aspect of a successful aquarium contributes—beautiful colors, fascinating behaviors, soothing gurgling sounds. In less-than-tropical climes, a tankful of tropical fish puts a bit of equatorial warmth into the chilliest environment, and, like flowering houseplants, a planted aquarium can soften the austerity of an urban environment. While it is undeniably ornamental, an aquarium can serve many other purposes in your home, and tropical fish are for many people the ideal choice in pets.

FISH AS PETS

Fish are the perfect pets for people with no-pets leases. Few rental units prohibit an aquarium, since fish don't shred furniture, urinate on floors, scratch woodwork, bark all night, or bite visiting landlords (well, as long as they keep their hands out of the tank!). They are the perfect neighbor-friendly pet, too.

With very few exceptions, a pet fish is not going to turn on family members, inflicting serious bites or scratches, and no mail carrier has ever been chased by a guppy. Your fish won't bring fleas and ticks into your home, and while there are a couple of bacteria that can be transmitted from fish to humans, there is nothing like the risk of diseases such as salmonellosis, listeriosis, ringworm, psittacosis, rabies, etc., that are communicable from other pets. Fish don't shed allergenic hair or dander, and even someone with acute allergies can view a tankful of fish with impunity.

In addition to being a safe choice as a child's pet, fish also are easy for children to care for, and maintaining an aquarium with adult supervision is a wonderful way for kids to learn the responsibilities and joys of companion animals. Often small children are frightened by even very small animals, but they are never afraid of fish "safely" trapped in a glass box of water.

And fish are extremely low-maintenance pets. They don't need to be walked or exercised. You don't have to housebreak them or train them to stay off the furniture. They won't scare off visitors, and if you leave them alone for a few days they won't wreck the place in protest. Even highly pedigreed specimens you are taking to a show never need bathing, grooming, or nail trimming.

BUT WHAT GOOD ARE FISH?

People used to playing catch with a dog or interacting with a garrulous parrot might wonder what enjoyment you can get from a bunch of fish swimming around a tank. Even an old tabby content to lie on your lap all day purring seems more interactive, and in a way this is true. The benefits of keeping fish, however, are many and varied, and they go far beyond the potential beauty of an aquarium, though the ornamental feature of a fish tank is not to be disparaged.

The relaxing and therapeutic value of an aquarium is well known, and it accounts for the popularity of aquariums in doctors' offices, hospitals, and nursing homes. An aquarium provides an air of serenity and encourages the viewer to relax and go with the flow. Beautiful, yes, but an aquarium has a *dynamic* beauty—animated color and gently rippling water. Most people find the sound of flowing water to be highly soothing, and watching the flow of water or bubbles in an aquarium can be almost mesmerizing. Even infants are often entranced by the peaceful but active movements of tropical fish.

While you won't be able to hold your fish on your lap or play fetch with them, keeping fish can be very much a hands-on hobby, offering many different opportunities for creative

Fish or Fishes?

What's the plural of fish, *fish* or *fishes*? Well, it's both. One way is to simply answer the question by choosing to use "fish" as both the singular and the plural, regardless of the context in which it appears. Another way—an arrangement used relatively rigidly by some writers, editors, and publishers, and one that you'll often see referred to as the right way in fish and aquarium books—is to use "fish" when only one species is meant and "fishes" when more than one species is meant. For example, under this arrangement you would say that five guppies and four goldfish are nine fishes, whereas eight goldfish alone are eight fish. Another way is to use "fishes" when the groups are viewed as dissimilar and "fish" when they are viewed as similar. There is no universally accepted rule, however, and if eight fish are all of the same species but each is a different breed or color or whatever, and you are trying to stress the differences among them, you could correctly say that they are eight fishes. Think of "fishes" as separating them for some reason, often in a comparison. For example, one might say, "North American fishes have different spawning challenges from those in South America," but "North American fish are not as endangered as North American amphibians."

interaction. Those with an artistic flair will find aquascaping—creating the layout of your tank—a fertile area for expression. Fishkeepers with a do-it-yourself bent will never be at a loss for tinkering projects. To people fascinated by natural history, the fish themselves will provide hours of enjoyment, and for many aquarists observing leads to various husbandry challenges such as the maintenance of difficult species, breeding fish, and even showing them in national and international arenas.

This leads to the educational possibilities an aquarium presents, and many schoolrooms, from elementary classrooms to high school and college science labs, boast one or more aquariums. Simple observation provides students with many topics of study—from ecology to ethology, from biochemistry to photoperiodicity, and from taxonomy to ontogeny, but even more possibilities arise from experimental projects, which can range from behavioral studies to genetics, microbiology to nutritional research, and comparative anatomy to histology.

WHAT'S THE CATCH?

Wow! Is there any downside to these practically perfect pets? Sure. I've already mentioned the minimal personal interaction you can have with fish. Fish are not, however, unaware of what goes on outside their tank, and they will learn to associate you with food, for example.

Many fish become hand tame and will eat from your fingers, while some of the larger species, especially cichlids and catfish, even come to appreciate a gentle rubdown or "scratch behind the gills."

Fish Out of Water?

Despite the common saying, many fish *do* spend time out of water, and not just in terms of jumping out of the water and splashing back down, which almost any fish will do. Amazon hatchetfish are actually capable of powered flight—to escape predators, they use powerful pectoral muscles to propel themselves farther than a mere leap could. A type of fish called the splash tetra shoots out of the water to lay its eggs on the underside of overhanging leaves. When the Asian climbing perch *Anabas testudineus* (below) finds itself in a pool that is drying up, it takes off over land to find a new home. African lungfish facing the same situation simply dig down into the mud, where they wait until the rainy season refills the pond. The mudskipper is a lively fish that spends much of its time on land—simply because it likes to! It slithers along the mud and up and over tree roots in search of tasty insects. It may seem weird to us, but to the question, "Are you a fish out of water?" many fish would simply answer, "Yes!"

Anabas testudineus, the climbing perch.

Much of the enjoyment, however, comes from watching the fish interact with each other. Common aquarium species exhibit such fascinating behaviors as breathing air, schooling maneuvers, often-rapid color changes, pecking orders, and territorial defense. The breeding behaviors of aquarium fish include live births, building nests made of bubbles, laying eggs out of the water, brooding eggs in the mouth, feeding the babies with slime from the parents' bodies, and the construction of sand and gravel towers to serve as nesting sites. Parental care among fish ranges from cannibalism to protracted protection of the young, and that care can be by the male, the female, or both, depending on species.

Perhaps the biggest negative that most aquarists will admit to is the addictiveness of fishkeeping. Once hooked, many people develop one of several conditions. Blank Wall Syndrome affects aquarists who cannot stand any blank spaces along the perimeter of the rooms in their home. Seemingly overnight, all such spaces are filled with fish tanks, often with *rows* of fish tanks and, in severe cases, *racks* of fish tanks, with aquariums lined both along the wall and up it in several tiers.

Not surprisingly, such people rarely have an unused aquarium, but they tend to accumulate tanks from places like garage sales, donations from family and friends, and spur-of-the-moment purchases. This usually leads to Empty Tank Syndrome, whose victims find it impossible to keep an empty aquarium; once in their possession, it must be filled with water and with fish.

Even aquarists with completely full walls and not even one empty tank are not safe. They are often afflicted with New Fish Syndrome, which is perhaps the most insidious of them all. People suffering from this condition will read about a species of fish or see one in the local fish store and become seized by an uncontrollable urge to have that fish. This affliction often strikes after terminal bouts with Blank Wall and Empty Tank syndromes, which means that the victims are forced to resort to shoehorning yet another aquarium into an overly crowded house or apartment.

For now, at least, you are safe from all this, and undoubtedly convinced it will never happen to you. (Don't say I didn't warn you, though!)

Chapter Checkout

- Fish are the natural choice, perfect pets for people with no-pets leases.
- While the interaction with fish is quite different from that with some other pets, an aquarium offers many therapeutic, decorative, educational, and avocational benefits.
- The main disadvantage to keeping tropical fish is that it can become an addiction.

Chapter 2

All I Want Is a Tank Full of Pretty Fish

Because of the fervent dedication of many aquarists, the needs of a new aquarium owner are often overlooked by people already well into fish. People who keep only rainbowfish or cichlids, or who specialize in large catfish or killifish or bettas, forget that they too usually started with just one tank with a variety of pretty fish in it. This book addresses the needs of the new aquarist.

What Lies Ahead

- research before making any purchases
- follow the advice in this book for guaranteed success

Of course you can enjoy keeping fish without specializing, without getting into rare species or breeding your fish. In fact, many aquarists never go beyond keeping an aquarium just as a thing of beauty and interest. On the other hand, many do go on to specialize, but it is best to get your feet wet with a simple but decorative tank. The important thing is to be *successful* with your first aquarium. An ornamental community tank is a great way to start, though there are other possibilities as well. There is an enormous amount you can learn about aquarium fish—in fact, even well-seasoned aquarists are continually learning new things. This means, however, that there is a lot of information around, and that can make it confusing for the newcomer.

DO YOUR HOMEWORK!

The single most important advice for a new aquarist is to learn as much as you can about any fish or group of fish *before* you make your purchase. Almost all tank failures can be traced to the owner's ignorance about one or more aspects of the fish they were trying to keep. Don't be afraid to ask questions of your fish and aquarium supplies dealer; good dealers will give you good answers.

Mastering husbandry techniques with small, hardy fish will give you the experience and knowledge to keep larger, rarer, or delicate species. Pictured is the catfish *Rhamdia quelen*.

Unfortunately, not all aquarium retailers are as informed as they should be, so you need to find answers yourself as well.

GUARANTEEING SUCCESS

When you begin to look into aquarium keeping, you will find an enormous amount of technology and information out there, along with a lot of prejudice and hot-tempered disagreement. In this book we will put all of that aside and present a simplified approach, an approach that leaves a lot of the details for you to investigate later—after you have had a successful first aquarium experience. This book minimizes the number of choices you have to make about your setup in order to maximize your success. In that regard it of course sacrifices completeness for simplicity—but it's a worthwhile tradeoff.

As just one example of this simplification, consider the air pump. The invention of small electric pumps to deliver air through plastic tubing to aquarium filters and other devices made a major difference to fishkeepers and opened up many new options. They became so basic to aquarium maintenance that many people cannot imagine a fish tank without one.

Air pumps, however, are not a completely unmixed blessing. While easy to maintain, they still require running tubing from pump to tank and using adjustable valves. There is nothing *wrong* with air pumps—in fact, I use them myself, despite what I'm about to say to you: don't bother with an air pump for your first tank. You don't need one, because today's filters and powerheads will provide all of the water movement and aeration your tank needs. You need the filter anyway, so the air pump becomes expendable. If you're absolutely dying to have a stream of bubbles rising in your tank, go ahead and get one; otherwise, save your money for more worthwhile aquarium expenditures—such as upgrading your heater or filter.

I won't fill this book up with an explanation like the foregoing for each of the things I choose to leave out, or for ignored procedures or techniques. It isn't likely that with my half a century of working with tropical fish I do not know about some device or practice you might come across or have recommended to you, so it is safe to assume that if it isn't in this book there is a good reason I chose to leave it out. This reason might not be anything other than my decision that the device or practice was either unnecessary or overly complicated for a first aquarium. I'm not saying you should *not* use such things. All I'm saying is that you don't *have* to.

The leaf fish *Monocirrhus polyacanthus* is a fascinating example of mimicry. Unfortunately, its absolute refusal to eat anything other than tiny living fish makes it a difficult species for the home aquarium.

You're not seeing things—this is a glass catfish, and yes, you can see into its body.

TIME OUT!

Now we come to a dilemma. I'm ready to start telling you about how to have that successful first fish tank, but you probably do not know very much about the kinds of fish you can keep. The problem is that you need to know something about the different types of fish and what they require before you decide about equipment, and you need to know something about equipment and husbandry to choose what kind of fish you want to have. This mutual interaction of your fish and your setup can become a real problem.

What's the solution? Read Part 4 now. Read it now to get an overview of the types of fish you can choose from and what their general characteristics and needs are. Then read the sections following this one, and read Part 4 again when you get to it in the normal order of the book.

Since the fish you choose can determine the equipment you need, and the equipment chosen can limit the fish that are suitable, you need an overview of the fish before you can start making choices. So sit back, relax, and read Part 4. Then go on to become a successful aquarist.

Chapter Checkout

- Do your homework! To be successful you must learn about a particular fish before buying any of that type.
- This book guarantees your success by narrowing down the choices you must make and avoiding discussion of unnecessary topics.
- Minimized choices allow you to start slowly, growing into the hobby gradually.
- The protocol in this book presents many choices made for you, often with extremely strong reasons. You should ignore advice from other quarters.
- You face a chicken-egg problem: you need to know about fish to choose a setup, but you need to understand setups to choose fish. Therefore:
  - Read the whole book before spending a cent.
  - Read Part 4 now, then return to this page and read through to the end.

Know Your Fish

Certain fish need certain types of setups, and certain setups are ideal for (or unsuitable for) certain types of fish. So how do you figure out what kind of setup and which fish you should get?

Well, the key to this chicken-or-the-egg problem is simply knowledge. If you understand the types of tanks you can have, and if you know something about the most common fish, you can make educated choices.

Please: read the *whole* book before you buy a single thing.

Otocinclus sp.

Chapter 3

Beating the Odds

Statistics are funny things. Depending on what you choose to portray, you can "prove" just about anything with them. This makes them meaningless unless you also investigate the causes behind the statistics. I remember in a psychology class being shown a graph of water temperatures versus number of drownings in Cayuga Lake, with a caption explaining that the statistics prove that warm water causes drownings, since the number of drownings rises significantly as water temperatures rise. Of course what was left out of the picture was the fact that the warmer the water, the more people can be found in Cayuga Lake. On a day like the one here above Cayuga Lake today—temperature 4°F (-16°C), moderate wind, light snow—*no one* is in or on the lake, drowning or not!

What Lies Ahead

- the common pitfalls that trap new hobbyists
- what you need to learn to avoid these pitfalls

Well, by similar illogical statistical interpretation, you are almost doomed to fail as a new aquarist, since a majority of people who start with tropical fish quickly leave the hobby. As with the drowning example, however, there's something left out of the picture.

WHY DO MANY NEW AQUARISTS QUICKLY BECOME EX-HOBBYISTS?

Many of the people who set out to become aquarists give it up within a year. Most of those who do are discouraged by failure, meaning their fish die. No, they decide, the aquarium hobby is too difficult. But it isn't! So why does this happen? Very often it happens simply because the new hobbyist lacks the information needed to succeed—or, equally common perhaps, the beginner is overwhelmed by an enormous volume of sometimes contradictory information and cannot see a clear path through it to success.

If we instead look at how many aquarists who have successful first tanks remain with the hobby, we see a big difference between them and the aquarists whose first tank is a failure. Most people who succeed with that first aquarium stick with the hobby. Okay, so you *aren't* doomed to failure, but how do you become one of those successful aquarists, and why do others fail?

The number of choices potential aquarists face can be sufficient to drive them from the hobby before they even begin! What tank should I get? What type of filter? What about lighting? What type of fish should I have? What foods are best? What about pH, hardness, and the nitrogen cycle—what are those? These and hundreds of other questions can turn what should be an enjoyable experience into a morass of indecision and frustration.

AVOIDING PITFALLS

The four most common causes of such failure and frustration are: the troublesome New Tank Syndrome, overfeeding your fish, overstocking and compatibility issues, and getting lost in all the available technology. Let's look at these four problems.

New Tank Syndrome

This all-too-common affliction results from ignorance of the details of tank cycling, but often new hobbyists are inundated with science to the point that they treat cycling as a mystical ritual based on principles beyond mortal comprehension, sometimes with disastrous results. In this book we'll cover only the very basic details—sufficient knowledge to correctly cycle a tank, but far short of enough for a degree in biochemistry!

What is tank cycling, anyway? Well, we'll cover it again later in this book, but for now let's just say that it is very important to stock a tank very slowly with fish, because it takes time for the biofilter to establish itself. And what's a biofilter? Again, there will be more later, but for now let's just say that a biofilter is used to turn the highly toxic wastes that fish produce into less harmful substances, and it can take up to two months to reach peak efficiency. What's important right now is that you recognize that failure to understand this process is a major cause of beginning aquarists' failure.

Overfeeding

Many more fish are killed with kindness than through negligence or malice. Unfortunately, advice for beginning aquarists is many times deficient in specifics and often potentially dangerous itself. Since I'd rather scare you into keeping your fish on a diet than lead you to overfeeding them, the advice in this book will seem extreme next to most. But go with it; your fish will thrive.

Overcrowding and Incompatibilities

One of the most common scenarios for a first tank is a 10-gallon (40-liter) aquarium with angelfish, neon tetras, and tiger barbs, and it's a long-term disaster from the word "go." Also common are a 5-gallon (19-liter) tank with 40 fish in it, or a tank of guppies and platies that is decimated overnight by the addition of a cute baby oscar. These unfortunately typical situations are all catastrophes waiting to happen, but they can easily be avoided—*if* beginning aquarists are sufficiently scared away from them. So be prepared to be scared!

Getting Tangled Up in Technology

There are some fish whose husbandry requires a very specific water chemistry, and there are many ways in which the chemistry of your aquarium water can be modified to provide an environment as close as possible to that of your fish's natural habitat. Likewise, there are many wondrous gadgets available to the aquarist today, and you can tinker with them to your heart's content (and your wallet's lament!), but the amount of equipment really needed to properly care for an aquarium is not that great.

Here's an analogy—what do you need to change a tire? Well, a shadetree mechanic might slip on his handy disposable coveralls and pull out his hydraulic jack, pneumatic tool with lug sockets, hubcap pry bar, rubber mallet, and wheel chucks. Someone else might do the job with a rock under a tire and a jack whose lever doubles as a pry bar and triples as lug wrench, then pound the hubcap back on

The Numbers Game

It is physically possible to cram an aquarium full of fish, with just enough water to wet them. The other end of this extreme would be a tank full of water with no fish in it. Where is the appropriate compromise?

Overcrowding is an especially dangerous practice, since it is not only bad for your fish itself but also increases the risk of disease, and it overloads the biofiltration capacities of your aquarium.

So be sure to stock your aquarium lightly.

with his fist. There's no doubt that the first method is in one sense "better," but when they're done it would be hard to tell the two jobs apart. And on a deserted road far from a garage full of tools, the second method would have an enormous advantage.

Well, if you become enamored with keeping fish and with the various pieces of equipment available to assist you in that endeavor, fine. Then you can have all the fancy, specialized, and esoteric toys you want, but for now we'll stick with the practical basics.

KISS

Our game plan here is to keep things as simple as possible and still give you a successful start as an aquarist. We could call it KISS—Keeping It Simple and Successful. Even within the simplified guidelines presented here, there are many options for the interested person to choose among for a first aquarium and to get started in the hobby the right way. If you succeed with your first aquarium by keeping it simple enough, the appeal that drew you to tropical fish in the first place will continue to grow stronger instead of petering out in the face of frustrating failure.

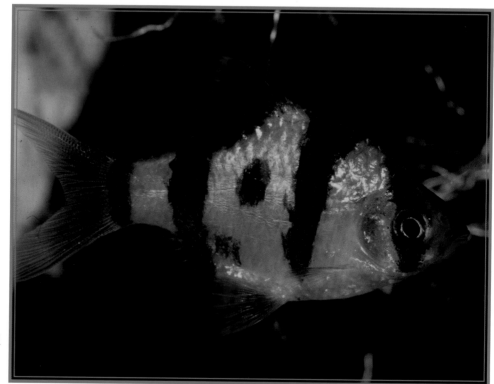

If you keep things simple when setting up your aquarium, you will succeed. Pictured is a tiger barb.

ARE YOU A CHEMIST?

If you are, you can skip to the next chapter. If you are not, then this little section is very important. There are three things for you to remember:

Chemists, not aquarists, work with chemicals. You should resist any advice that encourages you to treat your aquarium as part of a big chemistry set. Unless you have the training to know the attributes and interactions of all the chemicals you are adding, you cannot do so safely, and if you had that knowledge you wouldn't be adding them.

A healthy tank does not need any salt or other chemicals. A well-managed aquarium really has need for only one chemical treatment—removing the chlorine or chloramine added to municipal water supplies. This is a case where your water already has in it chemicals that can kill your fish, so you have to add something to neutralize those chemicals. If you have unchlorinated well water, however, the water from your tap should need no chemical adjustment. You do not need to constantly add different chemicals to your aquarium, and it will be much better off if you refrain from doing so.

You cannot manipulate just one water parameter; if you add chemicals to change one property of your water, other properties will also change. I'm not going to veer from the simple path we've set out on by going into a complex discussion of osmosis, cell membranes, and the complex chemistry of ionic solutions. I am simply going to point out that every chemical you add to your aquarium water puts stress on the fish in it, even if the chemical in itself is not toxic—or is even beneficial—to the fish. Some aquarium water is so loaded with unneeded and potentially harmful chemicals that it is amazing the fish survive—and often they don't. Don't put chemicals into your aquarium unless there is something wrong with that aquarium and you know exactly how the chemicals will fix it.

A LITTLE MORE SCIENCE

There are a few basic scientific principles that you must understand to be a successful aquarist. You do not, however, have to understand them in great depth, and you do not have to balance equations or follow complicated protocols. There are three essential principles you should understand as part of this section on avoiding pitfalls. You will probably not be surprised to hear that these scientific principles are heavily involved with the common pitfalls listed at the beginning of this chapter. By understanding the science behind them, you can avoid these pitfalls completely, putting you out of the statistics on failed aquarists.

Key to Success

Three Keys to Aquarium Chemicals
1. Few aquarists are chemists.
2. Adding chemicals often stresses fish.
3. An aquarium does not normally need to have any chemicals added.

What You Don't Know Can Kill Your Fish!

The worst problem that can arise in an aquarium is invisible, silent, odorless, and deadly. It's ammonia poisoning.

You must understand how to start and maintain a biofilter so that your fish will not be victims of ammonia.

So this simple scientific overview is a fitting finish to both this chapter on beating the aquaristic odds and to this first section of the book, which is meant to give you the background to decide whether aquarium keeping is for you.

Waste Buildup

The confines of a glass box do not really simulate fish's natural environment. The biggest problem for the fish is very easy to understand—there is nowhere for their wastes to go. After a while those wastes build up to levels at which it's almost as bad as if the fish were swimming in an unflushed toilet. There are, however, a few things we can do to vastly improve the conditions in an aquarium and make it habitable for a wide variety of species.

Waste Management

Most people think of feces (fish droppings) when they think of fish wastes, and removing the mulm that accumulates on the bottom of an aquarium provides improvement to both the aesthetics of the tank and the water conditions. Much more serious, however, is the unseen waste ammonia. This substance is produced by both fish and the bacteria that decompose fish wastes, uneaten food, and other organic substances in the water. Fish excrete ammonia both in their urine and directly into the water through their gills. In other words, the production of ammonia in an aquarium is unavoidable. You will find discussions in aquarium literature about the pH-dependent equilibrium between ammonia and ammonium, but hey! This isn't supposed to be Chem 101, right? All you have to know about ammonia is this: fish make ammonia, and ammonia kills.

Our goal, therefore, is to get rid of ammonia. Fortunately, certain species of bacteria that will grow in an aquarium environment love to eat ammonia. Unfortunately, what they do is change ammonia into nitrite, which is still very poisonous to fish. Fortunately, other species of bacteria that will grow in an aquarium environment love to eat nitrite and turn it into nitrate. And, fortunately again, the nitrate these bacteria produce is much less toxic to fish. In fact, nitrate can build up to a considerable concentration before fish start to suffer. Obviously, then, getting these helpful bacteria to grow in your aquarium is very important, and it is what is required to avoid the first pitfall, New Tank Syndrome. This is the basis for what is called biological filtration, or biofiltration for short. This and other types of filtration will be discussed in the next chapter.

Nutrient Export

The other aspect of waste management significant in aquarium husbandry is the removal of substances that are undesirable for reasons other than their toxicity to your fish. It may seem weird to talk about wastes and nutrients in the same breath, but in the natural cycle of life, one organism's waste is another's food. In fact, it is much more a network or a web than a cycle.

The two major nutrients of importance in an aquarium are nitrate, which we've already talked a bit about, and phosphate. The reason these two are significant is that they are both used by algae, and therefore proper nutrient export can avoid another common problem—one we can call Green Tank Syndrome. By removing nutrients from the system you can prevent algae from overrunning the tank, turning everything green. The easiest way to export nutrient wastes from your aquarium is to change some of the old water for fresh. If you remove half of the water, you remove half of the dissolved nutrients. And while you're removing that water

Large-bodied fish like this goldfish produce more waste than small fish, like dwarf cory catfish, for example.

you have a perfect opportunity to siphon out waste matter that might have collected in or on the substrate; since that waste matter is an important contributor of nutrients, you want to get it out of the aquarium.

EATING LIKE A FISH

Overfeeding is the second pitfall, and there are two bits of science to understand with respect to it.

Overfeeding the Tank

When fish overeat, they, like the rest of us, get fat. Obesity and fatty liver disease are problems no wild fish has to contend with, but many aquarium occupants do, and those conditions lead to health and reproductive problems. The greater threat, however, is the overfeeding of the aquarium itself. Huh?

The explanation is a single word: ammonia. Yep, it's bad enough when a fish eats some food, digests it, and excretes ammonia as a waste. At least the fish removes a lot of the nutrients from the food. It gets worse when the fish is given too much to eat, since it will put out a lot more waste in this case. But when you overfeed a tank, putting in more food than the fish can consume, the uneaten food rots, producing even more ammonia.

Eating Behavior

What we're concerned with right here is feeding behavior coupled with the physiological connections with that behavior. By understanding this biology, you can avoid a lot of overfeeding problems. There are two basic types of eating behavior among aquarium fish.

The first is a constant-snack mode. Fish that consume mostly plant material must "graze" pretty much constantly. Plants are much lower in protein than animals, so the fish have to eat a lot of this low-nutrient food. The digestive systems of these fish are designed to take in a constant stream of low-protein foods and are ill equipped to handle either large meals or meaty foods.

The majority of aquarium species, however, while constant snackers, are not herbivores but omnivorous micropredators, meaning they eat tiny animals like worms, bugs, and the like, along with some plant material. Small animals are high in protein, but they are low in volume, and they don't just sit around waiting to get eaten. So the fish that eat them get a nibble here and a nibble there, but it's hunt and pick all day. Their digestive systems are designed for a steady stream of tiny bits of meat.

The best way to feed all of these fish is to provide extremely tiny, extremely frequent meals. If you are able, six or seven meals per day is great, but anyone should be able to handle at least three—morning, when you come home from school or work, and shortly before bed. These meals should be not much bigger than infinitesimal in size, but we'll go over that in greater detail in a later section.

Adding live plants to your aquarium will help remove some of the harmful chemicals from the water. Your fish will also be more at ease, as plants provide good hiding places for them. Pictured is a swordtail, *Xiphophorus* sp.

The other type of kept fish is a large predator. These fish typically eat a huge meal on an occasional basis. That is, they'll swallow another fish that might be up to two-thirds their own size, then digest that for several days before feeding again. It is important to realize that this is not completely by choice. Even the fastest, fiercest, most ferocious predator has to work at it to catch its meal, and it has to be driven by sufficient hunger to make the chase worthwhile. Remember, predators' meals do their best to escape!

What this means for aquarium care is that these fish have a horrible tendency to overeat. When fed pellets or chunks of fish meat, these guys are all too willing to eat and eat and eat. They get very good at jumping excitedly every time you enter the room and looking at you with pleading eyes until you give in, but such overfeeding only leads to aquarium pollution and health problems for the fish.

Perhaps surprisingly, the best solution for these fish also is frequent small meals. In this case that translates into once or twice per day. An alternative that more closely mimics the natural situation is to feed larger meals two or three times a week, but that can make keeping the tank clean much more difficult, as large predatory fish produce copious wastes.

Some fish will prey on others. Pictured here is a *Xenetodon* needlefish and its meal.

SOCIAL ISSUES

The third pitfall we previously covered involved the problems associated with improper stocking of the aquarium—the One of Those and Those and Those Syndrome. It presents two distinct biological problems.

Glass Boxes

The first is that the best filtration and management practices in the world cannot change the fact that an aquarium can hold only so much water. It is therefore limited in both space and in the ability of the water to provide oxygen to the fish and to remove wastes from them. Even when not overcrowded to the point of asphyxiation, crowded fish are stressed fish, and disease, injury, and weakened immunities are the result.

Later on we'll take a look at some of the factors that determine just how many fish a given aquarium can properly support. Although this is one of the toughest areas of aquarium management to quantify, this book will provide several guidelines to help you understand this extremely important topic.

Animals in Those Glass Boxes

The second problem involves behavioral incompatibilities among the fish in a tank. These problems run from a situation in which one fish simply swallows another to one in which there is insufficient room for individual territories, and the fish are constantly fighting and injuring each other. It also includes cases where fish with extreme but opposite requirements are combined, to the obvious detriment of at least one species.

Unfortunately, while the first two pitfalls can be avoided by understanding a few basics of feeding and waste management, the two problems involved in stocking your aquarium are not as easily overcome. This is one of those areas where accomplished aquarists know intuitively how to proceed, but it is very difficult to impart this knowledge to someone just starting out.

Obviously, then, research is a key here. Part 4 of this book is designed to help you gain a feel for these topics so that you can make educated choices when stocking your tank with fish. Much of the information there will acquaint you with various types of fish and their different requirements, and a whole chapter is devoted just to the practical issues involved in determining the fish-carrying capacity of your tank.

I guarantee you that if you follow the advice given in those chapters, your aquarium will look empty compared to almost any other beginning aquarist's. But then a year or two from now you will still be enjoying fishkeeping and perhaps even expanding your collection with a tank you got at a bargain price at a garage sale run by some other aquarist.

Toilet Habits

Fish don't look for the nearest fireplug like a dog, or dig holes in litter like a cat, or stop in their tracks like a horse, or use one corner like a rabbit, or even just lift their tails out of the way like a bird—they just go when nature calls.

The reason for this, of course, is that they live suspended in the universal solvent—water. They can simply dump their wastes wherever they happen to be, and a moment later the wastes are dissipated.

In an aquarium, however, the wastes have nowhere to go.

Chapter Checkout

- Many new aquarists fail because of one or more of four common pitfalls:
  - New Tank Syndrome
  - overfeeding
  - overcrowding and incompatibilities
  - getting tangled up in technology
- Chemicals are not simple.
  - Chemists, not aquarists, work with chemicals.
  - Most chemicals are unnecessary for a healthy tank.
  - You cannot change just one chemical parameter of water.
- Just a little science is needed to avoid the four pitfalls. You must understand:
  - waste buildup, waste management, and nutrient export
  - fish eating behavior
  - fish social issues
  - how to keep things simple

Part 2: Sifting Through the Hardware

There is seemingly no end to the ingenuity of manufacturers of aquarium equipment, and a great many products are available, including both the useful and the decorative. Some might even seem frivolous, though one person's convenience is another's luxury. And, obviously, all this variety in equipment leads to a great variety in methods of setting up and maintaining an aquarium system.

The aquarium hobby has come a long way. When I started keeping fish in the middle of the last century, there were few choices and few options for setups. I remember when I had two types of fish food—granules that looked like toast crumbs and a green powder intended for mollies that was mostly dried, pulverized spinach, I think. For aquarium lighting we had tubular incandescent bulbs, and filtration was all air powered. Now it is hard to believe the diversity of supplies and equipment available for the aquarist. Diversity, however, creates complexity.

So here in Part 2 we will delineate the equipment you absolutely need to succeed. If you follow the advice in this book, you will not have many choices to make when you buy your supplies. But you will have success, and armed with that you will be able to try out the ever-growing panoply of equipment and accessories.

Chapter 4

What Do I Have to Have?

Walk into a typical fish store and you can be overwhelmed by the number and variety of pieces of equipment available to the aquarist. Not much of that equipment falls into the absolutely-must-have category, but some of it does. Here is my list of items that are either absolutely necessary or very worthwhile purchases indeed (even if they're optional); you can see how small a list it really is.

- Tank
- Stand
- Substrate and Decorations
- Cover and Light
- Heater and Thermometer
- Power Filter and Biofilter
- Water Test Kit(s)
- Aquarium Salt
- (Ich Medication)
- Bucket and Siphon Hose
- (Algae Scraper)

What Lies Ahead

- the necessary equipment for setting up and keeping an aquarium
- biological filtration

TANKS

Obviously you need the aquarium itself. You will find tanks that are made of glass and tanks that are made of acrylic. You will find standard rectangular aquariums in sizes from 2.5 gallons (10 liters) to 220 gallons (800 liters) and more, plus an assortment of bowfront, hexagonal, pentagonal, and other shapes in various sizes. Which should you choose?

Construction

Get a glass tank. Acrylic tanks have a lot of advantages (they're lighter and more resistant to jarring and shocks, for example) but also have disadvantages (higher cost and easier scratchability, for example), and for your first tank glass will suit you much better, if for no other reason than that it's cheaper.

Of course, if you already have access to an acrylic tank, it will work fine for your first tank. You will have to be very careful about scratching it, however. Scratches can be buffed out of plastic and not out of glass, but plastic is so much more susceptible to scratching than glass that you may have to make frequent use of this "advantage."

What Shape?

You should choose a rectangular aquarium. In addition to being less expensive on a capacity-for-capacity basis, rectangular tanks also are the most efficient in shape, since they maximize surface area. (Another drawback to other shapes is that they tend to be relatively quite deep, which makes it more difficult to maintain them and harder to find equipment to fit them.) Surface area is the most significant factor in determining the carrying capacity of an aquarium, since it is at the surface *and only at the surface* that gas exchange—oxygen in, carbon dioxide out—occurs. The total volume of the water held by a tank is of less importance than that tank's surface area in determining its suitability for housing fish. Let's look at a specific example.

No Bowls! Repeat: No Bowls!

Mythconception: Tropical fish can successfully be kept in a fish bowl.

Reality: A few species might *survive* in a bowl, but they will never *thrive* there.

In most cases keeping fish in a bowl is an act of cruelty.

The standard 15-gallon (60-liter) aquarium and the 20-gallon (80-liter) high tank have the same surface area, since both are 12 inches by 24 inches (30 cm x 60 cm). The 15 is 12 inches (30 cm) tall, and the 20-high is 16 inches (41 cm) tall. The gas exchange in both tanks is based on the 2 square feet (0.18 square meters) of surface area. In terms of volume into which wastes can dissolve, the 20-gallon tank does, of course, have 5 gallons (20 liters) more water. This is not significant, however, since in the absence of proper filtration and waste management, either tank can become lethal to the fish in a matter of days. The extra 5 gallons buys very little extra time. Significant increases in volume, however, can provide a safety buffer, to the point that a 75-gallon (285-liter) tank is actually easier to maintain than a 10-gallon (40-liter) aquarium. We'll take a closer look at this idea in a minute.

Consider the size and shape of the front viewing panel. Some tanks are very squat—low and wide. They are called "breeder tanks" because they offer maximum surface and bottom areas for a given volume and are of great utility. Tall, narrow tanks are called "show tanks" because they are aesthetically more pleasing. Now you can breed fish in show tanks, and many gorgeous ornamental aquariums are of breeder tank proportions, but the names reflect this general difference. Basically, the more square-like the front viewing glass, the more ornamental the tank seems. On the other hand, the more square-like the bottom panel of glass, the more efficient and practical the tank becomes.

There is an interesting contradiction here. One thing that makes people ooh and ah about an aquarium is the beautiful aquatic plants. Thus a planted tank is certainly more showy than a non-planted one. Show tanks, however, are less suitable for growing plants. The extra water depth means that if you want healthy plants you have to have high-intensity lighting and this lighting is very expensive. The low breeder tank sizes, however, are ideal for planted tanks; there is a large variety of 12-inch (30-cm) tall aquariums that allow you to have beautiful plants with a much less complicated lighting system.

Key to Success

The shape of an aquarium is more important than the number of gallons it holds.

What Size?

It might sound counterintuitive, but your chance of success is greater with a larger tank. While you probably wouldn't want to tackle an eighteen-wheeler before learning to drive a pickup, the opposite is true for aquariums, where the smaller versions are more difficult to handle. The reason for this is simple: the larger the aquarium, the more leeway you have in making mistakes. Remember that waste management is of primary concern. With a very large amount of water, you have longer to catch problems and correct them before they become catastrophes.

There is also a psychological factor. People naturally want a nice assortment of fish for aesthetic reasons, so there is a mental minimum in choosing the tank inhabitants. For many people, this minimum far exceeds the carrying capacity of the smaller tanks, but larger tanks provide enough room for almost anyone's idea of a basic assortment.

Larger tanks are superior in terms of temperature regulation also. Consider which cools off faster, a hot cup of coffee or a steaming bathtub. The coffee cup, of course. The science behind this intuitive answer is that surface area and volume are not in a linear relationship: a body loses heat through its surface, but the amount of heat it contains is a function of its volume. Thus the thermal stability of a large aquarium is many times greater than that of a small

Starter Kits

Mythconception: Buying an aquarium "starter kit" is always the best way to go about setting up your first aquarium.

Reality: Aquarium starter kits are typically based on too small a tank, and they rarely contain all of the equipment you need for a successful aquarium. At the same time, they might include unnecessary items. So although buying a starter kit might have the potential for saving you money, it doesn't always work out that way.

Avoiding Horrible Accidents

The worst type of makeshift tank stand is not the one that breaks when you fill the tank, crashing down and sending water and glass everywhere—it's one that *doesn't* do that!

Even very modest structures can support a lot of weight in direct vertical force, but lateral stresses will send them smashing to the floor. That lateral stress can be as simple as a toddler leaning against it or even a tiny shift in the house's structure. For safety's sake, use only stands designed specifically for the size tank you have.

aquarium, and very small tanks are downright precarious with regard to temperature regulation. A short power outage on a winter's night can chill a 10-gallon (40-liter) tank lethally, while a 150-gallon (600-liter) tank in the same room might suffer only a slight drop in temperature. Likewise, a stuck heater in the small tank will cook the fish rather quickly, but with the large tank you'd have considerable time to notice the problem before it reached deadly proportions.

When you couple all this with the safety buffer of the larger sizes in terms of waste management, you realize that maintaining a small aquarium requires considerable knowledge and skills but that even a complete beginner has a good chance of succeeding with a large tank. So how big is big enough? There is no set answer to that question, as there are so many factors involved—an experienced aquarist might keep a 5-gallon (20-liter) tank with three killifish in it successfully for years, while a newcomer might dump 100 fish into a 40-gallon (150-liter) tank and kill them all in short order. Given that all other things are equal, I would set the absolute minimum size of the tank that you as a beginner should obtain is 20 gallons (80 liters), but larger would be even better.

The very popular standard 55-gallon (200-liter) aquarium is not ideal from the fish's point of view, being a tall show-type tank, but it has a respectable volume, it really looks nice, and it is often available as a "combo special," being on sale with tank and full hood for a very reasonable price. In fact, it is often available cheaper than a 40-gallon (160-liter) tank. Likewise, a 10-gallon (40-liter) aquarium often costs less than a 5-gallon (20-liter) tank, but I do not recommend the very popular 10-gallon size; it's just not big enough.

Does that necessarily mean that you should not under any circumstances get a 10-gallon tank? Of course not. Some people might not have room for anything bigger or might even have picked a smaller tank to fill a particular niche in their home decoration scheme, and of course some people—I'm thinking here primarily of young people who want a tank badly but can't get their parents' agreement to go for more than a 10-gallon setup—aren't really in a position to go along with my bigger-is-better advice. Better that they should start their introduction to the hobby with a smaller tank than not get into it at all, as long as they realize that they're putting themselves at a serious disadvantage right from the start—and as long as they promise not to put more than six or seven small fish into it and also promise not to blame the tropical fish hobby for being "too hard to succeed with" if they fail.

My all-around choice for the best tank for a beginner is one of the least popular sizes. In fact you will probably have to order one, since very few stores stock it—it's a stock size, but one for which there is not a great demand; it also might cost more than the more popular 55-gallon size. That tank is the 50-gallon (200-liter), sometimes called the 50 breeder. It is 36 inches (91 cm) long, with the other two dimensions being 18 inches (46 cm). Can it be an ornamental tank? Well, I own one that has been in on-and-off use for going on four decades. For years it was a focal point in my dining room, and one of my daughters, for whom fish have no value other than decorative, considers it her second favorite of all my aquariums.

If a 50 is too big a tank for you, I would recommend the popular 29-gallon (110-liter) aquarium. In the same way that a 20-gallon high tank is a taller version of a 15-gallon, a 29 is a taller version of a 20-long—both tanks are 12 inches (30 cm) by 30 inches (75 cm), with the 20-long at 12 inches tall and the 29 at 18 inches (46 cm) tall. And, of course, you can go larger than a 50. The very popular 4-foot-long 75-gallon (285 liters) is an excellent choice, and so is the 6-foot-long 125-gallon (475-liter) tank.

WHAT DOES THE TANK GO ON?

The best support for an aquarium is a stand designed specifically for it. The worst is a table, bookshelf, or any other piece of furniture that was probably never designed to hold the weight a fish tank represents—which is about 10 pounds for every gallon of tank capacity.

You can see that we quickly get into some sizable weights. A 20-gallon tank stresses its support with about 200 pounds, while a 55-gallon weighs more than a quarter ton. Fish tanks will *fit* on lots of surfaces, but many of those surfaces will not be able to handle this kind of weight.

Commercial aquarium stands are designed to hold that much weight, to hold it level, and to hold up under moist conditions. They are available in both metal and wood, with the latter coming in a large variety of styles all the way up to

Your tank should go on a stand. Aquarium stands are built to hold the weight of a full tank; household furniture is not.

This loach, *Botia histrionica*, has slithered completely out of an uncovered aquarium. Be sure to cover your tanks and keep your fish inside them!

furniture-quality cabinets that not only support the tank luxuriously but also provide storage space under the tank for accessories and support equipment. You can also get matching wood canopies to serve as both tank cover and light fixture. Incidentally, there is a very practical reason for why it might be a good idea to buy both tank and stand as a unit: the tank can come with a long-time warranty, but the warranty might be void if you don't use the tank manufacturer's matching stand. Make sure you check with your dealer.

Different Tanks For Different Fish

Different fish appreciate different aspects of an aquarium's size and shape. To rapid-swimming fish like zebra danios, *Danio rerio*, straight swimming room is most important, so a long, low, narrow tank can suit them nicely. For cichlids and catfish that stake out a territory on the bottom, the base area is crucial, so low, wide, squat tanks are best. Vertically elongated species like angelfish need adequate height to develop and display their finnage, so they need tall aquariums. Standard aquarium sizes provide a variety of shapes to choose from.

Bare-Bottom Tank

My saying that gravel is optional might shock you. I remember the first aquarium I saw without gravel in it, when I was a boy. A friend of mine had the gravel-less aquarium in his bedroom. What shocked me was how beautiful it was! He had decorated the tank with rocks, mostly beautiful rose quartz. He had no plants, and he turned on the light only when he wanted to view the tank, so there were absolutely no algae growing on the beautiful translucent stone. It was a most unusual and unnatural design, but it had a great simple beauty.

In many cases, the only reasons to have gravel in your tank are as a substrate for live plants and for your own sense of aesthetics. Bare-bottom tanks are much easier to keep clean.

WHAT GOES ON THE TANK?

Your aquarium should be covered. The two most common tank coverings are plastic hoods and glass tops. Both have hinged access doors, and the hood has a glass strip where the light fixture installs.

These tops serve several functions. Most importantly, they keep the fish in the tank and other things (dust, peanut butter sandwiches, the family cat, etc.) out of it. Some fish are more likely to jump than others, but *any* fish can jump out of a tank. Many people get a false security from the bottom-hugging habits of certain species of fish. Unfortunately, many bottom dwellers are slitherers and climbers, adapted to move over and through objects on the bottom. This

A closeup of a natural color, epoxy-sealed aquarium gravel in which the pieces are of various sizes and colors.

How Much to Invest?

Let's be honest. You don't know when you begin whether you are going to stay in the tropical fish hobby. You don't want to invest a fortune in equipment, at least at first. But I'm saying that the 10-gallon tank too small. So...?

First, the tank itself is typically not the major cost of setting up an aquarium, even for very large, very expensive tanks.

Second, because the cost of a 10-gallon tank is so low to begin with, its resale value is practically nil, while used larger tanks are often in demand.

Last but not least, the cost of a 50-gallon (200-liter) tank is only a tiny fraction of the cost of a weekend on the ski slopes. It does not cost very much to get a good start in the hobby. So do yourself a favor—buy a large tank.

same behavior makes it very easy for them to maneuver through very small openings at the surface and out of the aquarium. Just remember that *any* fish can jump, crawl, or slither out.

WHAT GOES INTO THE TANK?

For the purposes of this discussion, we'll define the aquascape as everything in the tank except the water, equipment, and fish. There is great latitude in what you can include ornamentally in your aquarium, and very successful tanks are run with both absolutely no aquascaping and with an enormous amount of it. Let's look at the different possibilities.

Substrates

It is not necessary to have a substrate for most fish. Bare-bottomed tanks are very serviceable, though they leave something to be desired aesthetically. There are even several types of plants that prefer to grow unplanted, and these plants of course can be kept in bare-bottom tanks. Breeders often use bare bottoms because of the ease with which they can be vacuumed clean of debris. It is very important when using a substrate to clean it regularly to prevent it from becoming clogged with filth; that filth is a great contributor to the bioload of your aquarium.

The most common aquarium substrate is gravel. Sand is not acceptable for most applications for a variety of reasons, of which the major one is that it permits very little water circulation and encourages the formation of toxic anaerobic zones. Aquarium gravel is available in a variety of sizes and types, with a range of natural colors and a whole rainbow of dyed colors. While you may care about the color, for your fish the most important consideration is the grain size. The large spaces between the grains of very coarse gravel are traps for food and wastes—and sometimes even small fish! A medium gravel is generally best, while for a planted tank you might want a slightly smaller grain. Substrates such as glass chips may look nice, but they are a hazard to fish that root around at the bottom, since they may cut the fish's tender mouths, and they tend to pack very densely, creating the same types of problems as a sand bed. Aquarium gravel from your pet shop can be trusted to be inert and non-toxic.

Decorations

The ornaments in your tank can range from none to many, from completely natural to completely artificial. Your dealer will probably have a wide variety of rocks, driftwood, and manufactured decorations.

It is extremely important that any wood or rocks you put into your tank are safe for your fish. Be sure to check with your dealer that the pieces you wish to purchase are suitable for the type of tank you are setting up. Some stones are suitable only for marine or specialized setups, and driftwood can leach and tint the water amber.

Tank decor serves two functions—an aesthetic one for you and habitat for your fish. Paradoxically, fish that feel secure because they have sufficient hiding places will be more likely to stay out in view, while fish in a bare tank often try to hide in the corners of the aquarium all the time.

Although we often feel that fish feel most "at home" with live plants and natural objects like rocks and driftwood, the truth is that fish look at very different parameters. That is why you will find wild fish living in soda cans, old tires, and other debris, and this is also why aquarium fish take readily to such things as a "cave" made out of a hunk of PVC pipe or a "plant" made out of a handful of knitting yarn. A bushy fluorescent purple plastic plant can afford a fish the same degree of security as a healthy live aquatic plant. So the choice of decor is up to you: all natural, with gravel, rocks, driftwood, and perhaps live plants, or garishly gaudy, with dyed gravel, neon plastic plants, and molded ornaments of underwater castles, sunken ships, or even toxic waste barrels. As long as your fish have a place to hide and a decor that gives them enough of a sense of security, they will not care what provides those things.

Live plants, of course, make for a natural and beautiful aquarium. If you wish to have live plants and keep them in good condition, however, you will have to use stronger lighting than you'd use in a tank without live plants.

Some hobbyists like to build tanks that imitate the natural habitats in which fish are found. Others want sunken ships, bubbling treasure chests, and exploring divers. Choose whatever pleases you and whatever is safest for your fish.

LIGHTING STRATEGIES

Aquarium light fixtures range from a single plain fluorescent tube up to combination metal halide and very high output (VHO) fluorescents with concomitant very high price tags. Fortunately, for your first tank you can get away with the simpler equipment. We'll go over some details of aquarium lighting in the next chapter, but right now I'll tell you about the three types of lighting based on what sort of plantings you want.

Fish-Only Aquariums

An aquarium that is not going to house any live plants can be satisfactorily illuminated with a standard aquarium light fixture, usually housing a normal-output fluorescent tube that enhances the natural beauty and brilliance of fish. These fluorescent tubes are available in standard wattages, e.g., 40 watts for a 48-inch (122-cm) tube.

Low-Light Plant Aquarium

If you wish to have some live plants but don't wish to take out a second mortgage for your aquarium lights and for the electricity to run them, you can have a very attractive aquarium with light as low as 1.5 to 2 watts per gallon. This can be provided in most cases with dual-tube fluorescent fixtures, which are available to fit in the same space on the hood as the regular single-tube strip lights. You should use full-spectrum bulbs specifically designed for freshwater aquatic plant growth in this case.

There is a reliable trio of plants that will do very well in such a setup: Java moss, *Taxiphyllum barbieri* (previously called *Vesicularia dubyana*), which grows as a tangle of green stems, Java fern (*Microsorum* spp.), which has long, lanceolate leaves of dark green and grows on a rhizome stem that will attach to rocks or driftwood but should not be planted in typical fashion, and several species of *Anubias*, which are richly green and share the Java fern's dislike of being planted in the gravel. In fact such plants can be grown anywhere in the tank—on the bottom, on rocks, up on driftwood. In addition, plants of the genus *Cryptocoryne* will do well in some dual-tube systems, especially if the tank is not too deep, but they need to be planted in a substrate.

Hot and Cold

Several species of fish are very tolerant of temperature extremes. Some "tropical" species range naturally into temperate areas and can even survive outside until ice covers the pond. Other species are simply tough and hard to damage. The feisty convict cichlid is one of them. I have had convicts thrive in unheated tanks, and once, when the only spot I had for a tank was near the ceiling in a room where the temperature up there got about 95°F (35°C), the only fish I could imagine putting into it were a pair of convicts. They did very well; in fact, they spawned regularly and raised several broods of fry!

I don't recommend exposing your fish to temperature extremes, but I hope to illustrate that you don't have to fuss over a degree or two. Just keep the temperature in the upper 70s (about 24° to 26°C) and your fish should do well.

Aquatic Gardens

For more variety in aquatic plants, more light is needed—in some cases much more light. There are several ways to provide the necessary wattage, and we'll discuss them in the next chapter. This enhanced lighting is more expensive to purchase and to run, but it is possible to have a veritable garden in your tank with plants of all types, including flowering varieties and emergent plants, which grow right up out of the water. Spectacular gardens can be produced in uncovered tanks of almost any depth over which metal halide fixtures are hung.

Tanichthys albonubes.

HOW WARM IS "TROPICAL"?

The term "tropical fish" is used to cover a lot of different species with a lot of different requirements. The ever-popular white cloud, *Tanichthys albonubes,* prefers a temperature of about 70° to 72°F (21° to 22°C), while the small Amazon cichlid called the ram, *Mikrogeophagus ramirezi,* is comfortable at close to 90°F (32°C)! Most aquarium species, however, will do well between 76° and 80°F (24° and 27°C).

To maintain this temperature, you will need a reliable aquarium heater and a thermometer. Heaters are available in both hang-on and submersible models. The latter are slightly more expensive and tend also to be more reliable and accurate; since they can be placed anywhere in the aquarium, they allow much more flexibility in your setup. This type of heater attaches to the inside glass of the aquarium with suction cups and is completely submerged when operating. Placing the heater horizontally on the back glass, just above the gravel and right under your filter return, will maximize the mixing of the aquarium water by blending a hot zone around the heater with cooler water elsewhere.

Heaters come in various wattages. If you have a 50-gallon (200-liter) tank, a 150-watt heater should be sufficient. A 29-gallon (110-liter) tank requires a 100-watt heater. If the temperature in the room in which the tank is kept is likely to become rather cool, you will need a more powerful heater, perhaps even an additional heater. For example, you could put two 100-watt heaters on the 50, or two 75-watt units on the 29. Besides giving the extra wattage

Different filters contain different media. Research will explain the positives and negatives of each.

needed for maintaining the proper temperature in a cool room, this also provides a backup heater if one fails, and it makes it less likely that your fish will cook if you're using two heaters and one of them sticks in the "on" position.

An adequate thermometer is a stick-on type, which attaches to the outside of the glass. It shows the temperature by changes in color and is easily read, even from a distance. It's not the most accurate device, but your tank's temperature doesn't have to be highly precise, and with such a thermometer you can easily check on the tank's temperature every time you walk by, which will allow you to notice any problems early.

FILTRATION

I'll leave the details of different types of filters to the next chapter. Here we will look at the three types of filtration, what they do, and why you do or do not need them. All filtration involves passing the aquarium water through a medium of some kind. Depending on what happens within that medium, one or more types of filtration will occur.

Mechanical Filtration

Mechanical filtration is the physical trapping of pieces of dirt—suspended matter in the water that is unable to pass through the pores or fibers of the filter medium. This has the effect of removing these unsightly bits from the tank, but until the medium is cleaned or replaced, the material is still in the water and is therefore still contributing to the bioload—the waste production—of the tank. The function of mechanical filtration is largely aesthetic, although nutrient export does take place when the medium is refreshed.

The most common mechanical medium is polyester fiber, either pressed or woven into pads or in the form of a "fluff" of filter medium. As water passes through the fibers, the larger particles of dirt are trapped. Foam sponge blocks also are popular. When cut to fit a filter compartment exactly, the water is made to permeate the whole sponge, and the suspended matter will be left in the pores.

Chemical Filtration

Chemical filtration takes place at the molecular level. The most common medium is activated charcoal, which adsorbs an enormous variety of water contaminants. (Adsorption is the chemical attraction of molecules to the medium and their entrapment therein.) Carbon filtration can produce crystal-clear water and substantially reduce the pollutants in it, and it is frequently used with mechanical filtration—the carbon is sometimes manufactured right into the filter pad. Sounds great, doesn't it?

Well, it is! But there is a subtle hazard to using carbon, especially in your first tank: you can get to rely on it to cover sloppy maintenance. Use it wisely—as a backup to cover any mistakes you might make—but do not depend on it to keep your water safe for your fish. Activated carbon filtration is surely a marvelous technology. I personally almost never use it, however.

A mature biofilter will handle all the ammonia your fish release into the aquarium's water. Pictured is *Phenocogrammus interruptus*.

The reason is that I am a water-change fanatic, and I have a high-producing well that gives good-quality water. Why should I pay for carbon for my dozens of aquariums when I don't leave the water in the tanks long enough for it to be necessary? Still, activated carbon can be a very valuable tool.

As far as other chemical media are concerned, just avoid them. There are various media that will remove ammonia, nitrates, phosphates, and other substances from the water. They work very effectively in most cases. So why should you avoid them? Because you shouldn't need them. If you have problems with the aforementioned substances in your tank, you need to learn the cause of the problems and not just deal with the symptoms. Leave the chemical treatments alone until you have enough experience to be able to play around with them to get an idea of how effective they can be in case you run into a real emergency and are prevented for one reason or another from making a beneficial big water change.

Biological Filtration

I've saved biofiltration for last because it is the most important. It is also the hardest to understand and appreciate, largely because it is invisible.

It is biological filtration that enables your fish to survive. When you use mechanical or carbon filtration, there is usually a visible result—the tank and water look cleaner. (Of course, chemical filtration also removes some dissolved toxic materials from the water.) Biofiltration, however, removes substances we cannot see and replaces them with other substances we cannot see—and we cannot see the process itself at work. This filtration is performed by microscopic creatures living in microscopic pores in a biomedium, and it is vital to success with the aquarium; almost no tank will survive without proper biofiltration. Now all this talk is not to say that we cannot monitor biofiltration just because it's performed by creatures we can't see; we can monitor it by using test kits, which we'll get to in the next section of this chapter. For now, let's look at the basics of biofiltration.

Remember that biofiltration is bacterial filtration. That is, biofiltration removes harmful ammonia and nitrites from the aquarium water by culturing various bacteria that convert those substances into nitrates, which are much less directly harmful, in fact not harmful at all unless allowed to build up to high levels. These beneficial bacteria have very simple needs,

Keep Things Stable

If your water is not quite what your fish prefer, or if you want to keep a collection of fish with slightly different preferences, it is best to do nothing about your water chemistry. Fish are extremely adaptable to stable conditions, but they do not handle fluctuating water chemistry very well. If you keep your tank water optimized in terms of waste management, your fish will not mind terribly if the chemistry is a bit less than ideal, even though they might not show their best colors and they might not breed. Such a situation is better than to be constantly messing with various chemicals to try to "perfect" the water.

but they are extremely demanding about those needs.

THEY NEED OXYGEN

These microorganisms are aerobic, meaning they need a high-oxygen environment—the higher the better. This is especially important because if this need is not met, it is not merely the case that the bacteria will languish; they will also be replaced by anaerobic bacteria, which thrive in low- and no-oxygen environments and can produce deadly substances like hydrogen sulfide, which can kill all your fish (besides making your aquarium smell like rotten eggs!).

Testing your tank's water regularly will make sure ammonia and nitrites do not build up to dangerous levels.

At first, aquarium filters designed for biofiltration had high flow rates, which brought plenty of oxygenated water through the biomedium. This method is still used very successfully. Another method, however, was invented to make use of the much greater (20,000 times greater) capacity that air has over water for delivering oxygen.

What this means for biofiltration is that the enormous oxygen content of air can be used to bolster the oxygen in the water reaching the biofiltration bacteria. Remember that all gas exchange between air and water takes place at the air/water interface—the surface. Well, by vastly increasing the water's surface, we can greatly improve the oxygen available. This is done by various "wet-dry" technologies, which use a medium that is constantly sprayed with water but is not submersed in a container of water. Thus it is always moist, allowing the bacteria to grow, but it is also always covered by only a thin film of water, meaning that the oxygen-rich air is only a few molecules away from the bacterial colonies. This makes a phenomenal difference in the amount of medium needed to provide complete biofiltration for a given tank setup.

THEY NEED HOMES

The bacteria that take part in the cycling of nitrogenous materials do not live free-swimming in the water. Instead, they colonize surfaces. While they will certainly live on the sides of the aquarium and on plants and rocks, there will not be sufficient numbers of them to handle the wastes produced if that is their only place to grow. A biofilter is designed to house a biomedium, which is any porous material that provides a multitude of microscope surfaces the bacteria can colonize, and it situates this biomedium in a flow of oxygenated water from the aquarium. The best biomedia are those that provide maximal area for the bacteria to settle while still being open enough to prevent becoming clogged and thereby causing "channeling" of the flow of water to be filtered.

THEY NEED FOOD

Biofilter bacteria are hungry little guys. In fact, under good conditions, they will eat all of the ammonia and nitrites produced in your tank. If the amounts of these substances increase, the bacterial colonies will grow to match, provided that they have enough surface area to colonize; this is the whole idea behind tank cycling, getting the bacterial group to grow to sufficient size. We'll cover that in the chapter on cycling, but for now all you need to know is that any normal aquarium will provide plenty of yummy wastes for the bacterial colonies. Provided that the bacteria have sufficient area and oxygen, you won't have to worry about feeding them.

WATER TEST EQUIPMENT

It is possible to buy aquarium test equipment that can test for just about any imaginable water parameter. Some saltwater reef aquarists routinely test for a wide variety of solutes and properties—two dozen or more. Some of those aquarists are also chemists or could at least qualify as laboratory technicians. To be a successful freshwater fish keeper, you only have to know a few things about the makeup of your aquarium water, specifically the triplet of ammonia, nitrite, and nitrate. Different tests kits are available for testing for one, two, or more parameters in the same test.

Types of Tests

Aquarium test kits can be liquid reagent, solid (tablet) reagent, or test strips. The latter are often considered the least accurate, but if you take into account that an aquarist does *not* have to be a lab technician, the simple dip-it-and-read tests have a big advantage in that they're certainly the least expensive and easiest to use; also, they often have wider ranges than other test types. With these tests you just dip the test strip into a water sample, wait a designated time, and compare the strip to a color chart to read the result.

What About pH and Hardness?

Perhaps the most common unfortunate entanglement in technology for new aquarists involves another triplet of water parameters: pH, hardness, and alkalinity. Here now is where I am bucking tradition in choosing to leave a discussion of these three out of this beginner's guide. Simple definitions should illustrate why I am:

- The pH of a water sample is the negative log of the activity of the hydronium ion in solution, or pH = - log {H$^+$}.

- Hardness is a measure of the concentration of various divalent cations, primarily Ca^{++} and Mg^{++}.
- Alkalinity is a measure of the concentration of various anions that act as buffers of the pH, primarily carbonates and bicarbonates.

If those definitions mean something to you and if you want to, you can pursue these topics in another reference. If, however, those definitions don't seem familiar, you are better off concentrating on other aspects of aquarium keeping and leaving the chemistry for some later time. But I am going to have to have a promise from you. If you don't want to worry about the chemistry of your aquarium water (and I strongly recommend you don't worry about it), you must perform large water changes on a regular basis. There are many reasons for this, but the most significant is that regular water changes keep the chemistry of the water in your aquarium stable, and chemical stability is much more important to your fish than any particular chemical composition. In other words, the natural life processes that take place in any aquarium will, over time, change the water chemistry, but water changes maintain the water chemistry. It is okay for you not to know the exact chemistry of the water, but it is not okay for that chemistry to fluctuate wildly, as will happen if you don't keep up with water changes.

Many aquarists waste time monkeying around with water chemistry, which is almost never the cause of failure (though monkeying with water chemistry can itself be a cause of failure!), while they should be spending time on stocking issues, which are often the cause of failure.

Successfully changing your water's chemistry and maintaining it long term requires considerable knowledge and dedication. The whole process is a pain, one many aquarists are willing to endure for the purpose of keeping or breeding certain species, but one that is not necessary in 99 percent of the cases of someone just wanting to keep a simple fish tank. You see, most of the fish that won't do well without exact water conditions are not suitable for beginners for other reasons as well, and many of the species that need specific conditions to spawn successfully will do fine otherwise under a much broader range of conditions.

This means that providing a *steady* water chemistry is in most cases preferable to providing a *particular* water chemistry, and when it is a complicated procedure to provide that particular chemistry, your fish are likely to suffer one way or the other. If you avoid making necessary water changes because of the hassle of matching the water chemistries, they will suffer from pollution in their tank. If you keep up with the water changes but cut corners on the doctoring, they will suffer from fluctuating water chemistry. As I will point out several times throughout this book, fresh water of any non-extreme chemical makeup, coupled with regular large water changes, is what is best for your fish. You can use your tap water unless it has a terribly extreme

On Fish Diseases

Most fish diseases are:
- hard to diagnose
- hard to treat
- not very common

The exception is ich. That is the only disease you should diagnose and treat without expert help, and it's prevalent enough that you should have some ich medication on hand at all times, just in case.

Clean Water Means Happy Fish

Water straight out of your tap does not need any kind of filtration—it gets dirty in your tank. The idea is to keep it as close to its original condition as possible, through filtration and water changes.

chemistry. Most tap water is suitable in water chemistry for most common species of tropical fish. If you have reason to think your water is in the small majority that cannot sustain aquarium fish, you can have it tested at a local pet or fish store.

The Three N's: NH_3, NO_2^-, NO_3^-

Uh oh! Those symbols look like *real* chemistry! Yes, they do, but we've already covered them—those are the chemical formulas for ammonia (NH_3), nitrite (NO_2^-), and nitrate (NO_3^-). I threw them in just to see whether you're paying attention.

Testing for ammonia, nitrite, and nitrate is most important during tank cycling, of course, but you should initially test your water supply to practice using the kits and also to make sure you don't have any contaminations in your water to begin with. This may also alert you to the presence of chloramine in your water; perhaps you already know, from checking with your water supplier, whether yours contains chloramine.

Assuming you get straight zeroes for the three N's, your test kits will get a workout during tank cycling. Afterwards, they should be used regularly to check up on the system or to measure these important parameters at the first sign of fish distress.

WATER TREATMENTS

After all my preaching against using tonics and treatments, it is important to take a moment and point out that municipal water supplies add disinfectants needed to prevent horrible diseases in the people who drink the water. These chemicals, however, can kill fish. Unless you have a private well (and perhaps even if you do), your water supply will be chlorinated—disinfected with chlorine in some form, often chloramine. Chloramines are

Watch the Temperature

It is important to avoid pronounced temperature differences throughout your tank, even though natural bodies of water can have pronounced stratification of water temperature, with very warm water at the surface and cold water at the bottom. In the tropics, however, such stratification is minimal, since there are no cold bottoms. Most important, however, is that your fish are forced to visit the different strata of your aquarium much more rapidly than they would in a natural situation. Proper circulation from your filter should eliminate stratification.

Vacuuming your tank's substrate is a very important part of the water change.

particularly bad for fish because when water with chloramine in it is treated with a dechlorinator, the dechlorinator removes the chlorine but releases ammonia.

It is important that you contact your water company and find out what they add to the water. Make sure you tell them you are concerned about your tropical fish and find out all of the possible additions, including phosphates, to the water supply, not just what they are currently adding. Often the amount and types of disinfectant are adjusted because of changing seasons or conditions. If chlorination is all you will ever need to be concerned about, any sodium thiosulphate dechlorinator will work for you. If chloramines are a concern, you must be sure to buy a product specifically designed to neutralize these substances.

Make sure to follow dosage instructions. While it is true that these water treatments are fairly benign, they do add to the total dissolved substances in the water. As is always the case, plain water is best for your fish unless there is a specific need to add something else. Use just enough to do the job correctly.

To Carbon or Not to Carbon?

Activated carbon is a wonderful filter medium, providing chemical filtration of a variety of organic and mineral pollutants. It should never be used, however, to compensate for bad habits. Do not rely on carbon to make up for laxness in gravel vacuuming, filter cleaning, or water changes.

Don't Treat Symptoms, Eliminate Causes

Your dealer will certainly have one or more "miracle" products that instantly remove deadly ammonia from the water, although many dealers will recommend against their general use. The problem is that our concept of the "nitrogen cycle" is extremely myopic. You see, if you have rampant ammonia in your aquarium, something is very wrong, and that something is going to involve a lot more than just ammonia.

If you use these products and your ammonia tests return to normal, you might pat yourself on the back for being such a great aquarist, but in fact you will have done nothing to eliminate the original problem. Instead, you should first do a large water change to save the fish; this will also remove any toxins other than ammonia that also are being produced. Then identify what caused the problem—an unnoticed dead fish in the rocks, a plugged filter line, etc.

DO I NEED A MEDICINE CHEST?

I'm tempted to answer this section title's question with a simple "No!" and go on to the next. I believe more fish are killed by ignorant medicating of the tank than would ever have died from disease if they were left unmedicated. There isn't a medication in existence that will cure overcrowding or overfeeding, and these and other negligences are the primary causes of aquarium fish death in beginners' tanks.

An unfortunately common scenario is fish showing some stress, so the fishkeeper starts dumping in all sorts of nostrums, accomplishing nothing but stressing the fish further, often to the fatal point. What I'm about to say is *very* important:

When fish are ailing, a massive water change to *reduce* the concentration of junk in the water will be of real therapeutic value, and it's usually the best treatment.

Even in cases of infestations by disease organisms, massive water changes both invigorate the fish, increasing their ability to fight off the infection, and remove large numbers of the disease organisms. This is especially true of those that have a free-swimming stage before they attach to the fish. Often, however, the new aquarist is faced with fish that are not diseased but are suffering from overcrowding, overfeeding, or poor maintenance, and all of those conditions can be corrected best by massive water changes. *Adding* things to the tank in such cases only makes the problem much worse.

Now for that medicine chest—no, I didn't trick you. You do not need a stockpile of tonics and treatments, but there are two things you should have handy for a few specific situations that can arise.

Salt

The first is aquarium salt, or any regular salt (sodium chloride) that has not been treated with chemical additives such as anti-caking ingredients. Salt is a wonderful treatment for wounds, infections, and parasites. It stimulates the fish's production of natural protective slime, and it deters or kills many disease organisms. This doesn't mean you should start adding salt to your tank whenever your fish don't look right! If they have cottony white growths on them or open, gaping wounds, or creatures hanging from them, sucking their lifeblood, salt is a good treatment.

The best way to administer salt is to use a salt bath or dip. To do this, take a couple of cups of the aquarium water in a small container and add a tablespoon of salt. Mix it well, then net the afflicted fish and lower it, still in the net, into the salt bath. Keep a hand over the net to prevent the fish from jumping out. If the fish shows signs of distress (thrashing about), remove it immediately and dilute the bath with additional water from the tank before trying again. You can leave the fish in the bath for about two to five minutes, provided it does not show signs of distress. The dip can be repeated one to three times a day until the problem clears up. The salt can also be added to the tank in greatly reduced concentrations, but that is not the preferred method of treatment. If salt baths fail to cure the problem, you should consult a fish health professional.

Ich Medication

The other item you should have on hand is a proprietary ich medication. No, that's not *itch*, it's *ich*, and it's pronounced "ick." It's short for *Ichthyophthirius*, which is the name of the nasty protozoan that causes the disease. This parasite is the most common fish ailment encountered, and it makes a fish look as if it's covered with fine salt or sugar. It also kills fish—quickly.

The parasite has three distinct life phases. The organisms that are encysted on the fish's body or gills (the white spots) feed on their hosts. Then they drop off and form cysts on the substrate, inside of which they multiply. Finally the cysts burst open, and a horde of hungry free-swimming forms start hunting for a fish host. They attach to the poor fish, and the cycle begins anew. It is only in this free-swimming stage that medications are effective against the parasites.

There are many ways of treating ich, including several that use salt. The demise of the parasite can be hastened simply by raising the temperature of the water. The dividing line between lethal for the ich and lethal for your fish is fairly wide, but extremely warm water is not the safest treatment for an inexperienced aquarist to use. You definitely *should* raise the temperature of the tank a few degrees—even up to 85°F (29°C), but that alone is not sufficient to get rid of the ich.

Your dealer will probably have a choice of products designed to kill the ich organism. Since they can do that, however, only during the free-swimming part of the parasite's life cycle, you will have to treat the tank several times as more ickies become free swimming. The major problem with this method is that even products that claim to be safe can wreak havoc on the

The 20,000 Times Advantage

Biofiltration bacteria (and fish) need to live in water, into which oxygen does dissolve, but air has 20,000 times the oxygen of water! Aquarium water contains fewer than 10 parts per million (ppm) of dissolved oxygen. Our atmosphere, however, is about 20 percent oxygen, or 200,000 ppm. Air, therefore, contains more than 20,000 times the oxygen water contains. If this seems counterintuitive, consider that water is mostly just that—water! Many substances can dissolve in water, but only by fitting into the spaces between the water molecules. Air, on the other hand, is a mixture of gases. It doesn't have oxygen dissolved in it; it is one-fifth oxygen in its basic makeup. So how can aquatic organisms take advantage of the 20,000 times advantage of air over water? Simple: wet-dry!

biofilter bacteria. The ideal way of battling ich is to move all the fish (including ones that do not yet show signs of infection) to a spare bare aquarium for treatment, but you still have to treat your main tank or leave it without fish for a month, since the ich organisms can persist for three to four weeks without any fish to feed on. This is rarely a viable option, however.

If you have to treat your fish in the main tank, you have to keep checking the water for ammonia or nitrite and be prepared if the biofilter crashes to manage a recycling after treatment is finished. I cannot stress enough that eradicating ich in an established tank can be problematic, requiring several treatments and constant vigilance. Live plants may not survive the treatment, and the biofilter can become compromised or even killed off. In addition, the substrate and organic buildup in an aquarium can interfere with treatment, reducing the efficacy of the medication. Daily water changes with heavy vacuuming of the substrate are mandatory, with medication being added appropriately with the fresh water. Normally you can wipe out ich in about ten days this way.

The best solution here, however, is prevention—if you buy only healthy fish and properly quarantine new purchases, you are unlikely ever to have ich break out in your aquarium. We'll talk more about quarantine later in the book.

HOUSECLEANING EQUIPMENT

Most aquarium maintenance is taken care of through filtration and water changes, so the equipment for changing water is an important part of your aquarium technology.

Buckets and Hoses

We've discussed water changing in several contexts, and now it's time to go over the equipment needed to perform these changes. As usual, you can go high-tech or low-tech. The simple way is to use a bucket and hose. You siphon water into the bucket, dump it, and refill the tank with either the hose or the bucket.

You should have a minimum of two buckets marked for aquarium use only. Even one careless use of the aquarium equipment to wash the car or the floor could easily kill all your fish, since the residues of soaps and other cleaning chemicals are extremely persistent. Buy the buckets new and mark them boldly with permanent marker so that no one will make a mistake and use them. They will come in handy for many jobs other than water changes, among them being gravel washing; containers for acclimating/treating fish; someplace to hold wet rocks or decorations during cleanings; emergency quarters; convenient place to disassemble a messy filter, etc.

Using the same hose for your tank as for washing the car doesn't create any special contamination problem, but it is often best to have a hose reserved for your aquarium maintenance for convenience's sake. You should have the buckets in any case, but the hose can do double duty—you can siphon water out with the hose and then refill with the hose. All that is needed for this is a convenient place to which the water can drain and a suitable temperature-adjustable faucet to which it can attach. This is not only the lowest-tech method, it is probably the best.

Gravel-Cleaning Tubes

The only other thing you need is a gravel tube for vacuuming the bottom of your aquarium. Vacuuming the gravel or bottom should be part of any water change, and this is most easily accomplished with a gravel tube. Although it is indispensable for cleaning the gravel, it is also useful for cleaning bare-bottomed tanks, and it has the advantage that its decreased suction (in contrast to a plain siphon hose) makes it less likely a fish will be sucked into it, since all but the slowest can easily swim out of its way.

This simple device relies on basic fluid dynamics to decrease the suction so that the gravel is lifted and separated but not drawn into the hose, while the dirt trapped in it *is* liberated and sucked out into the hose. It seems almost like magic, but the principle behind the gravel tube is very simple. Water is drawn through the larger diameter tube into the smaller diameter hose, so the water travels faster down the hose to the drain and slower within the gravel tube. The device is designed so that the flow rate within the tube is insufficient to suck gravel into the hose but sufficient to suck the dirt particles in.

Getting Fancier

There are other devices that are supposed to make changing water easier, and they work with varying effectiveness. Most of them use water from a faucet to power the suction, so a great deal of fresh water is wasted down the drain to remove the old water from the tank. They are, however, especially useful when you have to drain water to a site higher than the location of the tank or when hauling water in buckets from its source to the tank is out of the question. My preference for such a situation, though, is to use a small submersible water pump.

ANYTHING ELSE?

A very handy device for aquarium maintenance is a scraper that holds a single-edged razor blade or has a hard plastic edge (for use with acrylic aquariums). A scraper of this kind makes quick work of any algae growing on the front glass. I am in favor of letting algae grow on the sides and back of a tank, unless those areas are meant for viewing as well. It's a natural-looking background, and it contributes a bit to the diet of the fish in the tank. It also helps keep algae from growing on the plants, rocks, and other ornaments, since a healthy mat of algae on the glass will absorb a lot of nutrients that otherwise would fuel algal growth elsewhere in the tank.

Another important use for this scraper is to periodically clean the underside of the glass on top of the tank. An accumulation of algae and/or calcium deposits is especially a problem with the narrow strip of glass on a hood. You will be amazed how much brighter the tank is after you clean the glass.

As for the outside of the tank, a soft cloth dipped in plain water is the only cleaning tool you should ever use. For particularly stubborn or greasy marks, wet the corner of a rag with vinegar or isopropyl (rubbing) alcohol. The fumes from the alcohol are not good for the fish, but they are not as toxic as the ammonia found in glass cleaners.

Chapter Checkout

The equipment you must have includes:
- tank—the bigger, the better
- stand—should be designed specifically for your aquarium
- substrate and decorations—can be natural or artificial
- cover and light—the type of tank you want will determine what kind of lighting you need
- heater and thermometer—smaller tanks require more watts per gallon
- power filter and biofilter—there are three types of filtration, with biofiltration the most important by far
- water test kits (ammonia, nitrite, nitrate)—you will need these most when cycling the aquarium
- aquarium salt—useful for treating many ailments
- (ich medication—good to have on hand at all times)
- bucket and siphon hose—or other water changing equipment
- (algae scraper—to keep the front glass clean)

Chapter 5

What Options Do I Have?

Okay, now that we've gone over in theory what equipment you need, let's take a look at the actual choices you have for filters and lighting systems.

What Lies Ahead

- filtration units
- types of lighting

FILTRATION DEVICES

First is the heart of the aquarium equipment—the filter. Remember that biofiltration is the most important, that all filters offer at least some mechanical filtration, and that some also allow chemical filtration as well.

Sponge Filters

Sponge filters are cheap, simple to maintain, and very efficient. They are ideal for use in fry-rearing tanks. They are also sin-ugly, and they have to be situated inside the tank. My fish room has dozens and dozens of sponge filters, but my decorative setups use none. They can be partially hidden by rockwork or plantings, but they are never going to be as unobtrusive as an outside filter can be. In addition, they are most useful for tanks of 20 gallons (75 to 80 liters) and under—tanks I do not recommend for you to start with. You can make up somewhat for their lack of capacity by using more than one in a big tank, but doing so of course compounds their ugliness.

The design of the sponge filter is simplicity itself. A hunk of foam sponge is fitted with a lift tube. If the filter is an air-driven type, an air supply line is connected to the lift tube and the rising bubbles draw water through the sponge and up the tube. Sponge filters can also be power driven, in which case a small pump called a powerhead is fitted to the top of the lift tube, and the pump sucks water up through the sponge and shoots it out into the aquarium.

A sponge filter: great for beneficial bacteria growth but not very pleasant to look at.

The principal function of these filters is biofiltration; the vast surface area of the myriad pores in the foam provide an enormous habitat for biofiltration bacteria. They also do a good job of mechanical filtration, since the flow of water draws debris onto and into the surface of the sponge. Maintaining these filters also is simple—when the flow becomes restricted, gently squeeze and rinse the sponge in a bucket of aquarium water until clean. You do this gently so as not

to squeeze out all the bacterial colonies, and you use aquarium water so that the temperature and chlorine of your tap water do not kill off the bacteria.

Undergravel Filters

I should say right at the start that I do not recommend an undergravel filter (UGF) as the filter choice for a first aquarium. This is not because they do not work; they do. It is because there are better biofilters available today, and I feel the problems associated with the UGF (more on this in a moment) are especially dangerous for new aquarists, who might not have the best maintenance skills. I myself use UGFs occasionally, but not very often. It may seem here that I am going against my pledge to not include certain information that will confuse the new hobbyist. I only explain it here because a UGF is such a commonly used piece of equipment that not including it would be somewhat of a disservice.

A UGF consists of one or more filter plates that cover the entire bottom of the tank. These plates are slotted or perforated, and they are raised so that there is a space under them. Fitted into the plates are lift tubes, which connect into this under-plate space. The entire filter plate should be covered with gravel to a depth of several inches. Since this operation must be done before anything else is put into the aquarium, a UGF is not a filter to add to an established tank. The lift tubes are fitted with airstones or powerheads, which draw water down through the gravel, through the slits in the plates, and into the empty space, then pull it up the tube and spew it back into the tank.

This action provides some mechanical filtration, as suspended particles are trapped in the upper layers of the gravel bed, but the primary function of a UGF, which was its unique contribution to aquarium technology, is that it turns the entire gravel bed into a biofilter. The constant flow of oxygenated water through the gravel permits biofiltration bacteria to colonize all of the surfaces of all of the pieces of gravel. As an added benefit, an undergravel filter effectively eliminates temperature strata in an aquarium through its ample mixing of water from all reaches of the tank.

Does the UGF have a downside? A couple. The first is dirt. Since the filter medium is the tank's gravel bed, you can't just lift the medium out and rinse it clean. This means that all of this organic material, while out of sight, is still contributing to the bioload of the tank, still producing ammonia and other waste products. In

Setting up a tank with a UGF, a good filter for use once you've gained some experience in the hobby. It's best to start with another type of filter.

addition, it can cause blockages of the system. What typically happens is that the space under the filter plate become clogged with detritus that has worked its way under the bed. When this happens, the entire tank must be dismantled, and it's a messy job.

In addition, bridging, or channeling, can occur. When the flow through the gravel is impeded in certain areas but continues elsewhere, unoxygenated zones develop. Anaerobic bacteria will grow in these areas; these bacteria do not assist in biofiltration, and they produce toxic substances like methane and hydrogen sulfide. A common cause of such a flow imbalance is having large rocks or other decorations sitting on a portion of the gravel bed, and it can also occur when fish dig down through the gravel, exposing a portion of the plate. In such a case, water flows very freely though the bare plate, leaving the amount of water flowing through the gravel greatly reduced. In both situations the problem increases over time, since areas with reduced water flow are more likely to become clogged with debris, sometimes shutting off the flow of water completely.

Can these problems be prevented? Proper maintenance of a UGF can greatly prolong the useful life of the system. Frequent (weekly or more often) deep vacuuming of the gravel bed during a water change will lift out most of the debris before it has a chance to work its way down into the gravel bed and under the filter. You should also occasionally run a narrow siphon (e.g., airline tubing) down the filter's lift tubes and draw out the water from under the plate. In this way you will prevent the buildup of sludge under the plate and lessen the tank's bioload considerably.

Another way of taking advantage of a UGF without the usual disadvantages is to use a reverse-flow system. A powerhead is fitted to each lift tube at its output, and its input is covered by a foam prefilter. In such a system, tank water is pulled through the foam and pumped down the tube and UP through the gravel bed. This greatly reduces the amount of detritus that can work its way down into the gravel. The only drawback is that the water flow is reduced, both because of the prefilter and because a powerhead's output is diminished considerably against pressure.

Other Inside Filters

There are other types of inside filters besides the sponge filters and undergravel filters we just discussed. One, the inside box filter, is actually the predecessor of the sponge filter. It consists of a plastic box with a slotted cover and a lift tube connected to a bottom plate. The filter media (usually floss and carbon) are placed on top of the plate, filling the box. The cover is then replaced, and an air supply provides bubbles up the lift tube, which draws water down through the medium and back up the tube. Except in rare and specialized cases, these filters are inferior to a sponge filter, and they suffer even more from a restricted filtration capacity and from the difficulty of hiding their ugliness.

Another type of inside filter is an internal power filter. These filters are very similar to the box filter in design, but they contain an integral submersible water pump that draws water

Hang-on filters are the best option for your first aquarium.

through the filter mechanically. The increased flow rate makes them much more efficient, and filters of a reasonable size can handle medium-sized tanks. Their main drawback is their inaccessibility; it is hard to check on the filter's functioning, and it is a mess to withdraw it to clean it, especially if you have it well hidden by the aquascaping. These filters are actually most popular among reptile and amphibian keepers, who often maintain tanks with low water levels. Most internal power filters can be placed horizontally rather than vertically in the tank—ideal for a turtle or frog tank only half full of water.

Then there are filters that are located outside the tank.

Hang-On Outside Filters

The hang-on outside filter is the most popular and versatile design, and it's the one I recommend for your first aquarium. This filter has undergone a lot of improvement since the early air-driven models, which were nothing more than a box filter hanging on the back of the tank. They were fed with siphon tubes, and an airlift returned water to the tank through the filter medium. Modern power filters use a water pump to draw water up from the tank and into the filter, where it flows through chambers of filter media and returns by gravity overflow to the tank.

Although there are models available that contain chambers into which you can heap the filter media of your choice, most filters today have modular filter components that you can mix and match and slide into the filter sections. That makes it much easier to service the filter,

Shutoff Valves

Make sure you have enough shutoff valves. They enable you to easily close down the water flow into and out of the filter so that it can removed for cleaning. If you cannot shut off the water flow, that simple job becomes very messy and frustrating.

and it also ensures that water will not find its way around the media instead of going through them, since the medium cartridges fit snugly into the compartments.

Usually a particular filter is available in a series of sizes, each successive one being both larger (and thus having more room for media) and more powerful (in having a stronger pump that delivers more gallons per hour). The idea here is that you can buy a filter sized to your particular aquarium. My suggestion is that you ignore such advice and choose one of the largest models. What?

First of all, you get more filtration for your dollar with the larger ones. Second, if you later upgrade to a larger tank, the larger model may still be adequate. Third, there is basically no such thing as too much filtration. An absolute minimum would be a unit that delivers a flow rate of five or six times the tank volume per hour, but ten times is even better. This is mainly because of biofiltration—more flow means more bacterial contact with more oxygenated water. It also improves the aeration of the water, making sure oxygen levels stay at optimum levels for the fish throughout the tank.

Last but not least, the ratings on most filters are nearly useless. Typically you might see something like "for aquariums of 10 to 60 gallons." A filter truly adequate for a 60-gallon (230-liter) tank would have a flow rate that would overpower a 10-gallon (40-liter) tank. Although I said that it's not possible to over-filter a tank, you also do not want the flow rate to be so powerful that it creates a whirlpool effect, with the fish being whipped around the tank all the time. The real problem, however, is that it is unlikely that the filter actually has an effective flow rate of 300 gallons per hour (gph), making it unsuitable for a 60-gallon tank. But even the gph rating can be misleading. The filter's *pump* may be rated at, say, 150 gph, but that doesn't mean that 150 gallons go through the filter every hour. Just pumping the water through the empty system will cut down on the flow; even the introduction of new media will reduce the flow, and as the filter gets dirty the flow decreases even more.

So what do you do? The solution is to buy the biggest and most powerful power filter you can. If you can hang it on the tank, it's probably not too big. I have very successfully used a spare 400-gph filter on a 20-gallon tank; when I no longer needed it there, the filter went back on a 55-gallon tank. The filter was slightly narrower than the back of the tank on which it hung, but it worked very well. An even better idea is to get *two* power filters, each big enough to handle the tank alone. Not only does this give you greatly improved filtration and aeration, but it also provides a backup if one filter suddenly breaks down, and it permits you to clean them on an alternating schedule, minimizing the loss of biofiltration capacity. Remember, there's no such thing as overfiltration, only underfiltration.

Canister Filters

Canister filters have some superior characteristics, but they are the most expensive way to go. One of their preferred characteristics is that they can be placed away from the aquarium (usually under it) and are connected to the tank by hoses. This means that the tank can be placed almost flush against the wall, since there only needs to be enough room for a couple of pieces of tubing behind it.

The major filtration advantage canister filters provide is that the water flows through them under pressure. This is because the filter is a closed system. Water is drawn from the tank and then flows into the filter, through the media, and back to the tank. It is driven by a water pump that, depending on the particular design, is either integral with the filter canister or plumbed into the system. This means that considerable power can be generated, which in turn means that the water is forced through the media under pressure, providing maximum filtration benefits. This also permits in some models the use of diatomaceous earth (a powder made up of diatom skeletons) as a filter medium; water will not really *flow* through it, but it can be *forced* through it under pressure. Diatomaceous earth filtration is meant as a temporary filter to "polish" the water—the diatomaceous earth cartridge is replaced by a regular mechanical medium for full-time use.

A canister filter setup housed in the stand underneath the aquarium.

Canister filters work well and are excellent for large aquariums. They don't do much that a couple of high-power outside power filters can't do, but they are very efficient filters, and many aquarists prefer them, despite their complexity.

Most of that complexity is simply plumbing, since you have to get water from the tank to the canister and back again. There are many options in how you set up a canister filter, which is why some of them do not include fittings, which have to be purchased separately. Fortunately, the major brands currently on the market all include fittings and tubing. Many canister filters have several options for the return, from simple tubing outlets to spray bars that diffuse the return flow over the entire surface of the tank.

Whatever filter you choose, if it does not have a true wet-dry option, you should use a sponge filter, add-on rotating contactor, or other biofilter in addition to it.

WET-DRY?

Recently "wet-dry" filters have enjoyed greater popularity for use with freshwater aquariums, although they have always been used mainly for marine aquariums.

Just what is wet-dry, anyway? Well, obviously, if filters are filtering aquarium water, they cannot be dry, but the name makes sense because these filters make use of a medium that is kept moist but not fully submerged in water. This is the "dry" part of the filtration process.

The purpose of this type of medium is to increase biofiltration, which it does significantly, because air has much more oxygen in it than the most highly oxygenated water does. With the vastly improved oxygen supply, many times the number of bacteria will grow in a given area, and they will process wastes at a much greater rate.

The design of wet-dry filters is quite varied, but they share the feature that somehow water is dripped, splashed, sprinkled, trickled, or sprayed onto a high-surface-area medium, through which it percolates before returning to the tank. Some power filters incorporate a wet-dry

Heavily planted tanks need stronger lighting than the type most beginner hobbyists initially buy. However, the plants recommended in this book that are perfect for beginners do not require such a high wattage.

section as the final stage, but there are also some that claim to do so and don't.

To be wet-dry, a filter must have an air-saturated medium that is not submerged—water must drip through it. Some of the designs for accomplishing this include:

Trickle Biomedia: Gravel is sometimes used in filters that have trays through which the water trickles, but the favorite medium here is pieces of ceramic or plastic shaped to maximize surface area. There are many different styles, some of them pretty costly, but in some instances cheaper alternatives, such as sand, provide even more in the way of microscopic surface area. The alternatives, however, may require a lot of maintenance, as they tend to clog much more easily and thus become ineffective.

Rotating Biological Contactors: This is the technical name for the rotating wheels of pleated material onto which pre-filtered water is sprayed. It is currently the ultimate in compact wet-dry technology, and a very small "biowheel" provides an enormous amount of biofiltration. These devices are available both as a part of power filters and as separate add-on units that can be used with a variety of filter types, or used alone with a powerhead and sponge prefilter.

LIGHTING SYSTEMS

Acronyms abound in aquarium lighting. The four most common types of systems are NO, VHO, PC, and MH, and you can also find combination fixtures such as MH/PC and MH/VHO. What does it all mean?

NO

Named by default after the invention of the other types of fluorescent lamps, NO is simply Normal Output lighting. NO tubes are available with a variety of spectral outputs, including full-spectrum types ideal for promoting plant growth. A 48-inch (122-cm) tube is 40 watts.

VHO

Very High Output bulbs resemble NO tubes, but they have guess what? Very high output! A 48-inch VHO lamp is 110 watts. These lamps require special ballasts and cannot be used in a regular fluorescent fixture. They create significantly more heat than normal output setups, which requires that steps be taken to prevent overheating of the aquarium.

PC

The desire to squeeze a lot of wattage into a small space led to the development of power compact fluorescents. PC tubes hook into the fixture at one end only, not at two. They typically have dual tubes, and they also require special ballasts and fixtures. A 48-inch PC tube can provide 96 watts.

MH

Metal halide lighting is the lighting preferred by many serious coral reef aquarists—and loved by their power companies. Such tanks with 1000 watts or more of MH bulbs on 12 hours a day mean not only a substantial investment in the lighting system and bulbs but also a small fortune for the day-to-day expenses of running the tank. The bulbs are available in a variety of types, rated by degrees Kelvin and usually ranging from about 5000K to over 10,000K. Although you might think so if you touched one, the designations do *not* indicate the running temperature of these bulbs. It is instead a measurement of the light spectrum produced. A 6500K bulb produces a spectrum like that of a black body heated to 6500K. But this is far from simple. For growing magnificent saltwater invertebrates, or for spectacular deepwater planted tanks, nothing beats MH, but it isn't the lighting for your first aquarium.

If you are going to keep only fish, the regular fluorescent bulb that comes with your light fixture should suffice. For low-light plants you will want at least to choose a full-spectrum bulb. It is best if you get experience with your first aquarium before tackling plants with high light requirements and the specialized equipment needed.

Chapter Checkout

- There are many different filtration devices available. I recommend a power filter and a biofilter—the biofilter being either a wet-dry component on the filter or a separate sponge filter.
    - sponge filters—simple, inexpensive, efficient—but also ugly and obtrusive (or at least unglamorous) in the tank
    - undergravel filters—great technology, but not the most recent technology and inferior to many others
    - inside filters—not as good as sponge filters, and no real benefit
    - power filters—excellent filtration for your money, and some have biofiltration capacity as well
    - canister filters—relatively expensive for a good one, but well worth it to some hobbyists
    - wet-dry filters—superb biofilters
    - Although biofilters usually maximize oxygen saturation, some focus instead on maximizing the effective micro-surface area of the medium. These "wet-wet" filters are less suited to use by beginning aquarists, however.
- Aquarium lighting is usually identified by acronym:
    - NO—Normal Output. Good for fish-only systems, and doubled full-spectrum bulbs for low-light plants or for very shallow planted tanks.
    - VHO—Very High Output. Good for many planted tanks.
    - PC—Power Compact. Like the VHO in application.
    - MH—Metal Halide. For deep planted tanks and luxuriant plant growth.

Chapter 6

What About Food?

Food is obviously a necessity for keeping fish. If you look at older aquarium books, you might see many pages devoted to collecting, raising, and preparing foods for your fish. Today, however, it is possible to raise and even breed fish completely with prepared foods you buy at your dealer. Those older texts spend a lot of time talking about enticing fish to eat dry foods, but the combination of nutrition and taste appeal of such foods today generates almost as much excitement in fish as live or frozen foods. The choice as well as the quality is truly impressive.

What Lies Ahead

- the types of food for your fish
- why "feeder fish" should be avoided

DRY PREPARED FOODS

There are literally hundreds of flake, tablet, and stick foods on the market. There are general types for mixtures of fishes, and there are formulations for carnivorous, herbivorous, marine, and bottom-feeding fish, as well as for specific fish such as cichlids, goldfish, koi, guppies, and bettas. There are foods that float and some that sink, and there even are others that are designed to sink very slowly, the object being to allow all types of fish to feed. Flake food typically contains a variety of types so that surface feeders and bottom feeders both get their share, while midwater feeders snatch the flakes as they sink.

It is best to offer a variety of foods, both to prevent boredom and to make sure that your fish are getting all the trace nutrients they need. You will probably find that your fish prefer one type of food to another. It is clear to me from their reaction that fish definitely respond to flavors and smells, and the different brands and different formulations definitely smell different from each other. Healthy fish will usually attack any food pretty greedily, however, and you do not have to allow yourself to be manipulated into always providing your fish's favorites—unless you want to.

Some fish will devour slices of blanched zucchini, like this *Ancistrus* catfish.

Dry foods come in many shapes and sizes. High-quality dry foods are great for your fish.

The Salad Bar

Herbivorous fish are ill equipped to handle a lot of meaty foods. Fortunately, there are many foods with a vegetable emphasis, and these foods should be the primary portion of the diet of such fish. In a mixed collection, things become more complicated. When the vegetarian in the bunch is a nocturnal suckermouth catfish, feeding sinking algae wafers after lights out is the best way to provide for its needs. When your herbivores are out there with the other fish, it is important to feed the plant-based foods first so that the herbivores, which are more likely to be attracted to them, can fill up before you feed the meaty foods. Such a situation, however, is always less than ideal, and it's something to keep in mind when selecting tankmates.

Which Is Which?

The following descriptions compare the major types of dry foods currently available. Very often a combination of types will work best for a mixed community of fish.

FLAKES

Food is flattened between rollers, producing very thin flakes of various sizes. The flakes can be fast or slow in sinking and can be crushed or even pulverized to feed the tiniest of fish. (Large flakes, however, are not much of a meal for very big fish, so feed these fish other foods.) Flakes are extremely adaptable and are available in an enormous variety of ingredients. Their flexibility allows fish to chew up or break pieces off large flakes. Flakes often are eaten by other fish before they reach bottom feeders; also, they tend to crumble when the fish eat, causing some to be wasted.

Why Do My Fish Nibble the Glass?

You might be concerned that you aren't feeding your fish enough because they nibble at the glass, or on plant leaves and other objects in the tank. This, however, is normal behavior, and the fish are actually eating, even though it looks as if they are munching on nothing. Their invisible-to-you snacks include algae and microscopic creatures, which grow in abundance in a healthy aquarium. It's not normally enough to completely sustain them, but it makes a fine between-meal treat.

PELLETS

Food is extruded as chunks or pellets, usually of a uniform size; they can be floating or sinking. There are many gradations of size, from micropellets for tiny fish all the way up to bean-sized pellets for very large fish. Because of their bite-size nature, there is very little waste with pellets. Large pellets can be given to fill up big fish's mouths, with smaller pellets then given for smaller fish in the same tank. The pellets are hard, so the fish they are intended for must have mouths big enough to swallow the pellets whole.

STICKS

Food is extruded like strands of spaghetti. Can be floating or sinking. Sticks currently are available only in medium and large sizes and therefore are suitable for large and very large fish only; they are excellent for jumbo fish that want a mouthful with every bite.

WAFERS

Food is pressed into disks of uniform size; the disks sink. Wafers of a few different sizes are available, but even the largest wafers are greedily picked at by small fish. Wafers, available in different formulations designed for herbivores and carnivores, have a high sensory appeal and typically are eaten greedily. They are excellent for use with bottom-feeding fish but not a good choice for most others.

By using a variety of brands and types, you can provide your fish with an interesting and nutritious diet. Although most fish foods are well fortified with vitamins and other essential trace nutrients, it is always possible that a particular food will be lacking in something—perhaps a nutrient that

Don't Neglect the Veggies!

In the wild, herbivorous fish grab every worm and crustacean they find among the plants and algae; this is an important protein source for them. In captivity, however, that excited enjoyment of an occasional fleshy tidbit can translate into serious health problems—even death. The digestive system of these fish is not designed to handle a steady diet of meat, and if they are fed such they will get sick. With herbivorous fish, use meaty foods as an occasional treat only.

has never even been studied to know how much fish need to have. By alternating among several types, you can keep your fish from getting tired of one kind, and you can make sure to cover any such nutritional loopholes as well.

FREEZE-DRIED FOODS

Freeze-dried foods are likely to get an enthusiastic response from your fish. They usually consist of a single food organism that has been freeze dried, though sometimes mixtures are available. Since they are so minimally processed, and since the processing is at low temperatures, such foods are very close to live foods in terms of taste appeal and nutrition. They make an excellent component of a healthy diet for your fish, and they are especially valuable when feeding growing youngsters.

Live tubifex worms in a worm feeder.

Tubifex

Tubifex worms are the granddaddy of freeze-dried fish foods. The worms form mats, and the freeze-dried mats are cut into cubes. You can press a cube against the glass, where it will stick—and be greedily attacked by the fish! These worms grow in sludge and muck, so they are often implicated in transmitting disease. This drawback is eliminated by some brands, which are sterilized to kill any pathogens present. Like all other strictly meaty foods, tubifex worms are bad as a steady major part of the diet of mainly herbivorous fish, which probably can't digest them properly.

Bloodworms

Actually the larvae of an insect (a midge fly), these organisms are a favorite treat of just about any fish, and the freeze-dried form does not lack in appeal. They wind up as individual worms that most fish can eat whole, but they are easily broken or even pulverized for smaller ones. But keep in mind that pulverizing freeze-dried and other dry foods tends to lead to overfeeding, so be careful if you use this technique.

Brine Shrimp

This perennial favorite of all fish makes a great freeze-dried meal. The shrimp tend to wind up as clumps, which can be broken up and dropped into the tank. As with the freeze-dried bloodworms, these clumps can be pulverized between thumb and finger, making a palatable powder even young fry will eat.

Plankton and Krill

Plankton and krill are among the most potent-smelling freeze-drieds, and boy, do fish ever go berserk for them—the water can boil with the feeding frenzy! Because they are freeze dried, you can crush or pulverize these foods before offering them, so that even the smallest fish can enjoy them.

FROZEN FOODS

Frozen foods are one step closer yet to live foods, since they still have the original moisture in them. This can be a drawback, since these foods are a bit messier than freeze-dried alternatives. The higher-quality brands, however, process the organisms so that there is minimal "juice" and waste.

Aside from the standard brine shrimp and bloodworms, you can get frozen *Daphnia* and special mixtures of different foods. These mixtures are especially popular for marine fish, for which there are formulations including such things as squid, sponge, and marine macroalgae, but freshwater fish enjoy them as well.

LIVE FOODS

Although you can provide all the nutritional needs of your pets with prepared foods, and although you can raise tankfuls of fish without using any live foods, there is no doubt that fish *love* live food. Many fish breeders use live foods to condition their fish, and millions upon

The Nose Knows...Or Does It?

Fish have a very good sense of smell—they can detect very small amounts of food and find it even in complete darkness. You can make use of this talent to trick them, however.

When your container of freeze-dried krill is down to a layer of fines (dust), dump a container of regular flake food into it. Shake gently to mix the krill particles in with the flakes, and let it sit for a few days. Your fish will react to the flakes much more enthusiastically than normal—unless, of course, you have highly unusual fish that like your flake food more than they like krill.

millions of captive-raised fish have been started on live baby brine shrimp.

Your dealer might have live tubifex worms, blackworms, or brine shrimp, and some aquarists go beyond and culture their own whiteworms, Grindal worms, vinegar eels, microworms, redworms, scuds, fruit flies, and other food animals. These are all fantastic fish foods, and I have nothing negative to say about their use. Feeding live foods, however, just isn't as easy to do for beginning hobbyists as feeding prepared foods is. If you are interested, you can research culturing techniques.

Bloodworms are a popular food because fish love them.

Soap Box Time!

There is, however, one soap box I must get up on for a minute. You should not feed "feeder fish" to your pets. Three species are commonly supplied as "feeders"—goldfish, guppies, and rosy red minnows. These fish are typically pathetic, housed in vastly overcrowded and underfiltered tanks, fed little or nothing, and usually full of disease and parasites. Doesn't sound appetizing, does it? The truth is, feeder fish kill a lot of aquarium specimens with introduced diseases and parasites, and they are not a good nutritional choice, given their usual sorry condition. And they are in almost every case unnecessary.

The fish that are often characterized as "needing" live fish in their diet are generally not candidates for a beginner's first tank, but I mention them here so that I can indicate that even these fish can usually be trained to take non-living foods, though you may have to use some live food at first. Crickets and earthworms will usually do the trick, making feeder fish unnecessary. If for some reason you must or want to feed live fish, you should raise your own. Fish you breed yourself and know to be well fed and free of disease make a much better choice as feeders than commercially available ones. Although guppies and other livebearers are the typical choice, any freely breeding species is a possibility, including blue gouramis, *Trichogaster trichopterus,* and convict cichlids, *Archocentrus nigrofasciatus.*

ALTERNATIVE FOODS

There are a few diehard aquarists who still mix up their own foods, blending various organisms and organs with other ingredients such as vegetables, vitamins, and gelatin and freezing the resultant mush. Such food often is excellent and well accepted by the fish. You can get into formulating your own foods after you've had your aquarium(s) a while if that's your

Many of the foods available freeze-dried also come frozen. You just pop the cube out of its wrapping and drop it into your tank. The fish will readily pick the cube apart as it thaws.

inclination, but for right now there's not much point in it, considering what's easily available to you.

Chapter Checkout

There are many types of foods to feed your fish.

- Dry prepared foods are available in either plant-based or animal-based formulations. You should feed a variety of them. They come in:
    - flakes
    - pellets
    - sticks
    - wafers
- Freeze-dried foods are enthusiastically eaten by most fish. Common types include:
    - tubifex worms
    - bloodworms
    - brine shrimp
    - plankton and krill
- Frozen foods are great treats for your fish. They are available as single organisms, e.g., brine shrimp, or as mixtures of different foods.

- Live foods are a special treat for any fish, though they are not necessary for most species.
    - Live foods your dealer might have:
        - tubifex worms
        - blackworms
        - brine shrimp
        - crickets
    - Live foods you can culture at home:
        - whiteworms
        - Grindal worms
        - vinegar eels
        - microworms
        - redworms
        - scuds
        - fruit flies
- Do not buy "feeder fish" to feed large fish.

Stay Away From "Feeder Fish"!

Mythconception: It is a good thing to feed live "feeder" fish to larger fish.

Reality: No fish suitable for a beginner require live fish as food. Commercially available feeder fish are usually loaded with parasites and diseases and are of inferior nutritive value.

Nannostomus eques relishing a live brine shrimp.

Chapter 7

There's Always an Easier Way

Even with the simple techniques presented here, there are easier ways of doing some things. Easier, though, does not necessarily mean better. In addition, making one aspect of aquarium care easier can increase the workload elsewhere. There is a certain amount of work necessary to maintain a minimally acceptable setup. For example, a 1000-gallon (4000-liter) tank with two small fish in it would not need much in the way of maintenance—it wouldn't even need a filtration system! It would, however, be far from satisfactory to most aquarists. In this chapter we'll look at a few simplifications that still produce satisfactory results.

What Lies Ahead

- ways to change water
- why you should change your aquarium's water

LOW TECH, HIGH LABOR

There is a way in which you can maintain an aquarium with the absolute minimum of filtration equipment as long as you are willing to substitute a considerable increase in maintenance effort. This system is to use water changes as the major (or only) filtration. Most setups can thrive with absolutely no filtration but with a 90-percent water change once or twice daily. Some commercial breeders use such a system. A hose is the only equipment needed, and your fish will do very well.

You will, of course, use a lot of water—but nothing else. The conservation of water should be a concern everywhere, and there are arid locations where such an approach is out of the question. To put things in perspective, however, let's look at how even a very extreme water change regimen would impact the average household. According to published estimates, if you have a 30-gallon (120-liter) tank and change 27 gallons (108 liters), or 90 percent of the tank's capacity, per day, this is equivalent to between four and seven flushes of a toilet. It also amounts to:

- about one-half of a shower
- about two-thirds of a clothes washer load
- less than five minutes of watering the lawn

Thus you can see that even at such a water change rate, this would be a very minor part of your household water usage. At a lesser rate of change, the usage is proportionately less. Furthermore, the water you remove from your aquarium does not have to be wasted down the drain. The "dirt" in the water—mostly fish wastes—is excellent plant fertilizer, so you can use it for watering houseplants, flower beds, gardens, or even the lawn. Many gardeners make "manure tea" by soaking manure in a barrel of water to provide a nutrient-rich liquid for watering their plants; well, aquarium water is also a nutrient-rich liquid, and you can drain it into a large barrel so you always have it on hand for your gardening chores. Of course for this we must assume that you live in a private house with some land around it, not an apartment. Obviously water-changing on a large scale is going to be less convenient for someone who doesn't have gardens and lawns and trees to expend his used aquarium water on.

Even if you simply put your old aquarium water down the drain, this water is easily recycled, since it is about the mildest thing flowing into your sewage treatment. It contains negligible solids, no harsh chemicals, and—compared to raw sewage—only small amounts of nitrogenous substances.

It is important to provide adequate aeration in the absence of full filtration, since the water movement usually supplied by the filter will be absent. Powerheads are a convenient way to do this, but airstones will also work.

Hobbyists with many tanks have devised simpler ways to stay on top of their water changes, ways that take a fraction of the time that changes with the bucket-and-hose method take. Pictured is the pencilfish *Nannostomus unifasciatus*.

LOW TECH, LOW LABOR

To manage aquarium wastes with little technology *and* little labor, some aquarists maintain very heavily planted, very lightly stocked tanks. When the primary function of an aquarium is as a water garden, the fish become secondary, and only a few small animals are kept. This means both that there is very little fish waste compared to a regular tank and that there are plenty of plants to utilize as fertilizer the small amount of waste that is produced.

The downside to this approach is that it is much easier to keep most fish than most plants, and the technology you save on massive filtration is more than made up for by massive lighting systems and perhaps carbon dioxide supplementation. Keep in mind that the type of tanks I am talking about here contain hundreds of plants and a few fish; dropping a half dozen bunches of plants into your tank does not count.

This is a low-tech method that turns out to be rather complicated, since in every aspect *except* filtration, planted tanks of this type are a rather advanced part of the hobby.

NO-TECH, NO LABOR

No tech, no labor? I'm not joking, but I am cheating a little with the use of the word "no." I'm talking here about two systems that, once set up, require practically no equipment or labor to maintain.

Different Filters

Do not confuse drip-overflow systems with a central filtration system, which uses the same type of plumbing. In a central system, however, the overflow does not go to a drain, but to a sump and filtration system, from which it is pumped back to the supply fittings for the tanks. Here one giant filter takes care of all the tanks, which share the same water. There are many advantages and disadvantages to such a system, but, obviously, you won't be using one on your first aquarium.

Flow-Through System

The first is a flow-through water system, which is basically a constant water change system. The tank is fitted with an overflow drain that flows when the water reaches a certain level. It is also fitted with a water supply outlet, which provides a steady stream of aquarium-ready water. You can see that the drain will always be flowing at the same rate as that of the water flowing into the tank. With sufficient flow, there is no need for any additional filtration or aeration.

Such a setup is typically found in commercial operations, but it is often used in a modified form as a drip overflow system by home aquarists with several tanks.

Drip-Overflow System

The only difference here is that the water flows through the system at a much slower rate. Instead of making up for a filtration system, it serves as an automatic water-changing system. Each aquarium still has a filter, but the water is kept fresh without periodic changes.

There are available devices that hang on the tank and accomplish the same thing without overflows or drilling holes in the tank for plumbing. These devices are water-powered and use the flow of water into the tank to also generate a siphon. One hose brings water from the tap to the tank while the other removes the surplus water to keep the tank from overflowing. These devices, therefore, use a lot of extra water just to power the siphon. They can be very useful, however, and can be moved from tank to tank to keep on a regular water change regimen.

NATURAL LIGHTING

In this case we focus on lighting, not on filtration. Despite the elaborate metal halide systems some aquarists use, the sun's light has yet to be duplicated. Aquatic plants do extremely well under natural lighting, and water depth is of little consequence—after all, sunlight travels 93 million miles to reach the earth, so what's a few inches more? How, then, can you utilize this wonderful free light source?

I have seen a few setups in which an aquarium is situated directly beneath a skylight, but this is not usually possible. Unless the tank is up at the ceiling, the light from a skylight will be quite diffuse and of little value for growing plants. A greenhouse full of aquaria is another possibility, but usually using sunlight requires growing the aquatic plants outdoors.

The problem is that even if you live in a warm enough climate, outdoors in the sun is not a good spot for an aquarium. Even a very large one will quickly overheat on a sunny day, and you'll wind up with fish stew and steamed greens instead of a lush planted fish tank. And, when it rains, the tank will overflow, and your fish will be lost. Outdoor fish pools and ponds are a possibility, and in most areas the summers are warm enough for hardy tropical species. Many aquarists do enjoy growing aquarium plants in outdoor ponds in the summer.

But what about growing aquatic plants in a sunny window? Locating a tank in front of a window is generally *not* a good idea (see the next chapter), but it can be done successfully with extra effort. This is another one of those cases in which simplifying one aspect of aquarium maintenance certainly complicates others. Even the lighting itself is problematic, since it comes from the side rather than from above. You cannot turn your aquarium regularly the way you do with a houseplant to keep it growing uniformly.

Some aquarists compromise and put a planted tank where it will receive a few hours of sunlight per day indirectly from a window. That eliminates most of the overheating worry and reduces the chance of unwanted algal growth, but you can still wind up with the plants growing sideways. I bring up this example more to discourage you from trying it than to recommend it; it seems like a good idea, but it has many inherent problems.

TIME FOR A CHANGE

We're well into the book now. Have you noticed a theme or two so far? Over and over I've mentioned water changes as the best, easiest, simplest way to prevent or remedy a long list of

Plants will thrive in sunlight, and aquatic plants are no different. However, extended exposure to the sun's rays can overheat your fish and cause an algae bloom.

Summer Vacation for Your Fish?

One summer when I was a kid, I took a few black mollies and put them into a plastic wading pool in the back yard (this was in New Jersey). Within no time the water was like pea soup with algae, and I got busy with summer things. Once in a while I'd catch a glimpse of black in the pool.

When the weather started to cool in the fall, I drained the pool and netted out the fish. And netted out the fish. And netted out the fish! I had dozens of the largest, most beautiful mollies I'd ever seen. The combination of the huge volume of water, plentiful food (mostly algae and mosquito larvae—two of the mollies' favorites), and warm sunshine gave this Northern boy a taste of what Florida fish farms can do.

problems. I've also already admitted that I'm a water-changing fanatic. I am this way because water changes work. There is good reason behind my mania. Water changes are the ultimate easier way, easier than using a bunch of equipment, easier than monkeying with chemicals, easier than measuring and dosing, etc.

Back in the Dark Ages when I started with tropical fish, the common wisdom was that the older the water was in your tank, the better. The only reason fish even survived is that by having old water and undisturbed tanks, we also tended to have functioning biofilters on the plants and in the gravel without knowing it. If we set up a new tank and moved fish into it, they often died. You see—new water kills!

Of course, now we know that we were delivering those poor fish a double whammy. They had adapted slowly to increasing quantities of pollutants, particularly nitrates, that accumulated in the never-changed tanks, so when we greatly freshened their water it was an enormous shock, even though the water was vastly superior. At the same time, a new tank had no biofilter established, so ammonia began to accumulate the instant the fish were added. This was a recipe for disaster, of course.

I'm telling you all this to demonstrate that I once believed that water changes were unnecessary, even bad. What changed my mind? Water changes! I found that when I paid attention to biofiltration and performed lots of large water changes to remove nitrates and other pollutants, my fish thrived as they never had before. I was spawning fish I'd never even been able to keep before. Moreover, even though I have hard, basic water, I was able to keep and breed some species that come from soft, acidic habitats. But what really convinced me was the fish themselves and their reaction to the water changes—they love 'em!

It's possible to begin to imagine what it must be like for fish in a tank. Such a mental exercise can help you realize the importance of changing water.

The Stinky Stuffy Room

Try this analogy on for size. You and your family or friends have to move into a room with sealed door and windows. There is a bathroom, but the toilet empties into a big pit under the floor, into which you also scrape any leftovers from your meals, which are delivered regularly and consist of your favorite foods in great quantity. Several fans suck the air through charcoal filters to absorb odors, then they blow the air around the room, and there is a small vent in the ceiling to allow some air exchange. How long do you think it would be before the room was uninhabitable? How soon before that would you become uncomfortable? How much would you think people in the room would offer just to have a window opened, let alone the pit cleaned out?

It is important for you to realize that this scenario differs from the aquarium situation in a very significant way—the smells and fumes that would drive you out of that room would be harmless to a large extent. Yes, the ammonia would burn your eyes if you got close to the pit, and there could even be some hazardous fumes produced down there, but by and large the problem would be one of being grossed out, not injured. In an aquarium, however, the fish are trapped in the pit! They swim in, breathe, and drink water saturated with their own wastes. Their skin and gills are burned by the ammonia. Nitrites enter their bloodstreams and cause brown blood disease—death by asphyxiation no matter how much oxygen is available. An equivalent in the stinky room scenario would be to add a poorly tuned lawnmower engine spewing carbon monoxide into the room through the vent.

One more analogy!

Trichogaster lerrii.

The Solidifying Cage

Imagine a single large fish trapped in a mesh cage suspended in its home river. It cannot move very far in any direction, but the water flows through the cage unimpeded. Obviously, this is not much different from the fish's being loose in the river, at least in terms of waste management.

Now suppose that the mesh of the cage sides begins to thicken slowly, with the spaces being filled in solidly. As time progresses, less and less water flows through the cage. Now the animal's wastes begin to accumulate before they are washed away, and soon the fish is constantly bathed in water that has a significant pollution level compared to the river water. Finally a point is reached where the water flow is so reduced that the wastes accumulate to the lethal point, and the fish dies.

Less-active fish, like this kuhli loach, produce a smaller bioload than more-active fish.

We could keep the fish alive for a while longer even in a completely solid cage by using filtration, especially biofiltration. But think how much better it would be if we could just knock out a few of the plugs from the mesh! A small flow would refresh the water inside the cage, and an even larger flow would make the filtration unnecessary again. Well, it's the same in an aquarium. Unless you have a flow-through system, which is very much like the cage with

the plugs knocked out, the "flow" through your tank is periodic—it occurs only during water changes. The closer those changes are to each other, the more like a true flow it will be.

Chapter Checkout

Various maintenance techniques have different strengths and weaknesses. This chapter covers some of the major choices you have regarding filtration and water changes as well as lighting.

Key to Success

Your fish will thrive if you think of your filtration system as a temporary fix between water changes.

- Low Tech, High Labor
    - little or no filtration
    - complete water change once or twice daily
    - aeration and water movement is extremely important
- Low Tech, Low Labor
    - heavy planting, light stocking of fish
    - an aquatic garden, rather than a fish tank
- No-Tech, No Labor
    - flow-through system
        - constant water changing
        - no filtration, aeration, or filtration is necessary
    - drip-overflow system
        - slower rate of flow
        - filtration is used, but water changes are automatic
- Natural Lighting
    - sometimes useful for indoor aquaria
    - more complicated than it seems at first
    - more often used with outdoor setups
- Water Changes
    - Are the best, easiest, simplest way to prevent or remedy a long list of problems.
    - Ultimately the easiest method of aquarium maintenance.
    - Fish love them.
    - Imagine yourself in a sealed room with your own wastes.
    - Think of your aquarium as a temporary vessel for water between changes.

Part 3

Time to Get Wet!

Okay! Enough talk. Time to set up that aquarium. In this part of the book we'll cover the mechanics of setting up your tank, from placing the aquarium all the way up through cycling and maintenance.

Chapter 8

Situating the Tank

Filled aquariums are not safely portable. You can't move one around the room to check out how it looks in different spots, as you can with a vase, or even a sofa. Once an aquarium is set up, the only way to move it is to empty it and tear it down completely. Therefore choosing where to put your tank and getting it right the first time is of high priority.

What Lies Ahead

- where not to place your aquarium
- considerations to take into account when placing your aquarium

BAD SPOTS

Let's start with places *not* to put the tank. I'll assume I don't have to mention obvious bad choices such as in front of the closet door or at the foot of the stairs, but there are some much less obviously bad spots, such as:

- In front of windows or near exterior doors—high temperatures in such locations can bake your fish, and cold drafts can easily overwhelm your aquarium's heater.
- Next to interior doors—you must be careful in such locations to avoid a design that permits the door to open into or even jostle the tank, which can result in breakage or in overstressing the fish.
- Near heat or air conditioning units or vents, or on a porch or in a room subject to extreme temperature variations—again, temperature extremes must be avoided. Temperature regulation in an aquarium depends on fairly consistent ambient conditions.

Certain areas of the home will stress your fish. Decide on a quiet spot where you can sit down and enjoy the tank's beauty.

- In the kitchen—a kitchen is less than ideal because of the grease, smoke, and other fumes. The bigger and better ventilated the kitchen is, the better it gets as a location for an aquarium, but it generally can be improved upon.
- On or over appliances like televisions or stereos—aside from the potential for water spills to destroy your expensive electronics, such locations are typically both unstable and subject to intense heating. Don't risk your fish or your equipment.

BALANCING ACCESSIBILITY AND FISH

You want the tank where it is both easy to care for and able to be maximally enjoyed by you and your family. On the other hand, you don't want so much traffic and other activity going by the tank that the fish are perpetually hiding. Some fish cannot be perturbed even by activity *inside* their tanks (large cichlids often find such intrusions a diverting challenge!), while others will zip behind the plants or decorations every time someone passes the front glass.

An aquarium can be a focal showpiece in a room, and a large tank can serve as a room divider. Most fish will adapt to having people passing by the tank frequently, but locations such as hallways that are too busy are typically bad for viewing the tank as well. Whether meant to be viewed while you are seated or standing, the aquarium should be passively prominent—it should be in a spot where you can relax and enjoy it. You don't want it where it will be difficult to work on the tank—too high, wedged in between furniture, etc.—but you also do not want it to be a hindrance to normal traffic and activity patterns in the room. In addition, the tank should be accessible to the necessary electrical and plumbing utilities, but that gets us into the next section.

ENGINEERING CONSIDERATIONS

No, don't worry, we're not going to get out the blueprints and hard hats. You have three important design concerns when choosing your tank's location, however.

Keeping the Tank on the Same Floor of the House

Since you are choosing a permanent location for your aquarium, it would be nice if it doesn't crash through to the basement or into your downstairs neighbor's living room. Remember that a 50-gallon tank tips the scales at about a quarter ton, and a 135-gallon beauty will strain your floors with almost 1400 pounds.

Most floors will support most normal-size aquariums, but if you have any doubts you should check with a professional contractor or engineer, who can examine your situation and tell you whether you will need to reinforce the floor. Whenever possible, an aquarium should be located *across* several floor joists, not on one or between two; that is, it should run perpendicular to the joists, not parallel to them. This distributes the considerable weight over several joists and can prevent sagging floors—or worse!

If the floor joists are accessible from below, they can be reinforced with braces or with telescoping floor jacks. Of course, if you have a finished basement and are placing the aquarium there on a concrete slab, you can in most cases have as big a tank as you wish without any fear of cave-ins.

Electrical Safety

The use of electrical appliances around water is inherently dangerous and potentially fatal. Building codes require GFI (ground fault interrupting) devices in kitchens, bathrooms, and pool houses—places where people use both electricity and water in close proximity. Unlike conventional protection, which cuts the power only when a certain amperage is exceeded, GFIs will also cut off the flow of electricity if they sense a leakage of electricity from the normal circuit. In other words, while a regular circuit breaker is inactive until too much electricity starts flowing through it, a GFI breaker will also trip if the amount of electricity flowing into the circuit is not the same as that flowing back through the same circuit to the system's ground. In such a case, the power is flowing somewhere else—the ground fault. If that improper ground happens to be via you while you're standing in a puddle of water and touching the faulty appliance, the speed and sensitivity of the GFI device is all that stands between you and electrocution.

A GFI device or outlet is one of the most important pieces of equipment you need. Water and electricity are otherwise a very dangerous combination.

All aquarium equipment should therefore be protected by GFI circuit breakers or individual GFI outlets, and the tank should be grounded. A glass box full of water is not naturally grounded the way a kitchen range or a swimming pool is. This means that power leakage from a faulty aquarium appliance into the water will not trip the GFI until something grounds the water—and that "something" is typically a grounded aquarist touching the water. Fortunately, it is an easy matter to provide a continuous ground to your aquarium with the use of a grounding rod. This is simply a titanium spoke inserted into the tank and wired to your house's electrical ground, thereby making a permanent ground. Now any power leakage into the tank has an immediate source to ground, and the GFI will trip. Grounding probes are available from your dealer.

The absolutely minimal electrical requirement for a single aquarium is to provide sockets to plug in three pieces of equipment—light, heater, filter. Depending on your setup, it could be considerably more. You should *not* use multiple taps, extension cords, or similar devices. Power strips are okay, provided you do not exceed their rating and don't string them together. Many people find it convenient to have the filter and heater plugged into a single strip, with the light plugged into another; that way, they can easily switch them off when doing water changes without losing the tank light. Leaving the filter running dry can damage the motor, and if the heater tube is exposed to the air while it is on, it will break when water hits the hot glass.

One last precaution is to put drip loops on all electrical cords. In the event that water gets onto a wire, it will flow down to the low point on the loop and drop off instead of flowing into the electrical outlet.

Where's the Sink?

The time to see whether you have a hose long enough to reach from a sink to your tank is *before* you fill it for the first time. You can, of course, use buckets to carry water to your tank, but besides being messier, that gets old *very* fast. The same goes for removing water from your tank—you can drain it into buckets, but it is much easier to siphon it directly into a drain or out the window into a flowerbed.

What if you have to dechlorinate the water? How can you then use a hose to fill the tank? Just place the appropriate amount of dechlorinator into the tank as you begin to refill it. The water spray will keep the water mixing, allowing the chemical to make contact with the chlorine in the water.

What if you don't have a drain situated lower than the aquarium? Well, first, perhaps you do. You don't have to use a sink drain—you might be able to drain into a toilet or a floor drain. If not, you'll need to use a pump—either a water-powered siphon or a small electric water pump.

By eliminating bad locations for your aquarium and indicating what the minimum facilities are, we have defined good locations for it, but the most important thing is to select from those places the spot where you will get the most enjoyment from your fish tank.

Chapter Checkout

Bad spots for your tank are:
* in front of windows or near exterior doors
* next to interior doors
* where temperature variation is extreme
* in the kitchen
* on or over appliances

Engineering Considerations
* The weight of an aquarium may require reinforcement of the floor.
* Use GFI protection and ground the tank.
* Do not overload outlets.
* Use drip loops on all cords.
* You aquarium should be convenient to a water supply and a drain to facilitate water changes.

Chapter 9

Fitting and Filling the Tank

Now that you've picked the right spot for your tank, you're ready to set it up. Don't get too excited when I tell you that the first thing you must do is fill the tank—you're then going to drain it right away.

What Lies Ahead

- make sure your tank is clean and level
- how to fill your tank properly

LEVEL AND RINSE

Once it's securely on the stand, you need to make sure the tank is level. Use a carpenter's level to check the level left to right and front to back. A nonlevel tank will be subject to leaks and breakage, and it will also have an uneven water line, which can interfere with your filter's operation. Often a lack of levelness that shows up when you're checking the aquarium results from a lack of levelness in the stand or the floor.

Now it's time to fill it for the first time. This is just to rinse out any dirt or dust that the tank has picked up and to check for leaks. Use cold tap water and fill the tank slowly, checking the seams for any sign of water seeping through. This also gives you a last chance to make sure you've picked the perfect spot, so step back and take a look at the filled tank—imagine it full of plants and fish. Just right? Good, drain it empty.

GRAVEL PLACEMENT

The gravel for your tank should be rinsed to remove the dust from shipping. Different types of gravel can vary greatly in the amount of dust they contain, but all of them should be rinsed clean. The easiest way to do this is in a bucket outside your dwelling. You'll need your two aquarium buckets. Turn on the garden hose and put the output end into an empty bucket. Slowly pour in a few inches of gravel, letting any dust or debris get carried away in the overflow as the gravel settles to the bottom. Give it a gentle stir with your hand, then pour off the water and dump the clean gravel into the second bucket. Repeat this process until all of the gravel has been rinsed. If for some reason you can't do your rinsing outside, you have to be much more careful, as you don't want to slop water all over the place. And since you'd then have to be doing your rinsing in a sink or bathtub, you'd also have to be careful not to let any loose gravel scratch the sink or bathtub's finish. Moving the bucket over the drain area while gravel is trapped under it can put some wicked scratches in even very durable sinks and tubs.

Now you have a bucket of wet gravel, and you have to turn it into the base for your fabulous aquascaping. If you're not using an undergravel filter, start by dumping the gravel into the tank, then smooth it level with your hand. If you're using an undergravel filter (though, again, I don't recommend one for first-timers), you would of

Is Everything on the Level?

Water seeks its own level. This means that if your tank is trimmed in plastic, as many of them are, you can use the bottom trim to double-check that everything is level. As you begin filling the tank, the water should come up to the bottom trim at the same time everywhere. If the front shows a water line but the back doesn't, your tank is tipping forward. If one side shows water but not the other, and the front has an angled water level from one end to the other, then your tank is leaning to one side. Correct any leveling problem before continuing to fill the tank. You should avoid using anything too easily compressible as shims; wooden shims work well enough.

course have to put the filter plate(s) over the bottom of the tank before adding the gravel. A flat gravel bed is perfectly serviceable, but it leaves a lot to be desired. First of all, if you slope it downward from back to front, detritus will tend to accumulate down front, where it is easiest to see and siphon out. If you are using live plants, this also provides the deepest substrate in the rear, where your largest plants probably will be. A nice effect is to also slope the gravel upwards from the center of the tank to the sides, making a bowl-shaped center section. Of course, all of this shaping will, over time, yield to the law of gravity (and gravel-moving fish) and tend to flatten out. Incidentally, gravel scratches glass easily and acrylic even more easily, so be careful when you're pushing it around the tank; loose particles adhering to your hands can do damage.

The leveling out of the gravel can be prevented by using rocks to terrace it. Slate is especially good for this, and it can be used either horizontally, by building up retaining walls by laying thin strips one on top of the other, or vertically, by standing strips of slate of about the same width on edge across the tank. Long strips will yield an angular setup, but short chunks can be arranged in a curved pattern. If you want to get really fancy (and permanent) about this, you can dry-fit the pieces of stone and silicone them together with aquarium sealant. Do this at least a couple of days before you set up the tank so that the silicone will be cured before any water is involved.

INANIMATE ORNAMENTS

Now it is time to place any rocks, driftwood, or other decorations. Be creative, but make sure all arrangements are sturdy. Silicone is once again very useful to bind dry pieces in a stable arrangement, though it is useless if the pieces are wet. You can silicone together different components like rock and wood—you can even glue objects to the tank glass. The silicone you use has to be the aquarium-safe type sold in aquarium stores; don't use silicone not specifically rated for aquarium use, as it often has chemicals in it to prevent the growth of mold and mildew, and these chemicals can be toxic to fish.

Plastic plants can be added now, but it is best to treat them as live plants and wait to place them until the tank is partially full of water. The reason for this is that without the water to buoy them up, their branches and stems will simply flop down, and it will be impossible to see the final visual effect of their placement.

FILLING THE TANK

After you've gone to all that trouble to carefully arrange the gravel, if you just start filling the tank with water you're likely to destroy your hard work. So instead take a bowl or small tub and place it on top of the gravel, and pour (or hose) the water into this. The container will absorb the force of the water and help to protect your arrangement.

Drifting Driftwood

Some driftwood sinks, but most will float until it is waterlogged. This type is often attached to a slate base, but the base is very often of insufficient weight to keep the wood from bobbing to the surface, even when covered with gravel. When you are first setting up a tank, it is an easy matter to use some silicone aquarium adhesive to attach the driftwood to the bottom to keep it in place before adding the gravel.

Do You Know Where Your Aquarium Has Been?

I once set up two aquariums, and since I had just gotten a new ammonia test kit, I decided to check it out before I added any fish. I did not, however, get the expected zero reading!

A complete water change solved the problem, but I wanted to know what was going on. I did some research and discovered that the tanks had been stored in a warehouse that had also housed some pigeons. The dried droppings had been wiped out of the tanks, but enough ammonia had remained, even after a quick rinse, to be at a dangerous level. So be sure to rinse well any aquarium you purchase..

I recommend that you fill the tank in stages. Stop when the tank is one-third to one-half full and examine it closely to be sure that everything is as you want it. It is much easier to rearrange things at this point than after the tank is full. Aside from the aesthetics of your aquascaping, check that equipment such as heaters, filters, and filter tubes are unobstructed. These things can be hidden by rocks, plants, or other ornaments, but they should not be blocked. The heater should not have objects touching it, and filter tubes should be situated so that they have unimpeded water flow.

Planting

Now is also the time to place your plants, if you are using them.

UNPLANTED PLANTS

Java moss, Java fern, and *Anubias* should be loosely anchored to objects with thread or rubber bands, not planted in the gravel. Obviously, floating plants are not planted either. If you are including bottom plants as well, make sure that you do not have so many floating ones that they block the light from the others.

"BUNCH" PLANTS

Many of the plants sold in bunches of stems will root if planted, though most will also do fine if simply left to sink to the bottom. Hornwort, *Ceratophyllum demersum*, however, will not root even if you anchor it in the gravel.

You should never plant the bunch the way it comes. The stems will be held together with either a metal strip or rubber bands; there will be no circulation around them if they are left that way, and the plants will rot. Separate the stems and plant them individually—they'll look better, too. The best effect is to plant one or more bunches as individual stems placed about one-quarter to one-half inch apart.

ROOTED PLANTS

The easiest way to plant rooted plants is to grab the plant right at the crown, then gently depress it into the gravel a few inches from where you want to place it. With the crown at the correct planting level, draw the plant through the gravel to its final spot. This spreads the roots and gives the plant a firm anchor.

Anubias nana.

Ceratophyllum demersum.

To get maximum plant growth, aquatic gardeners use—in addition to high-intensity lighting—special substrate fertilizers, bottom heaters, CO_2 supplementation, and mineral supplements. You will, however, get decent growth without these extras, provided that you have adequate light and that you plant heavily. It is necessary to have a relatively heavy planting to take up nutrients before algae can get the upper hand.

The Final Fill

Once your plants are set, you are ready to fill the tank to the top—which you should do carefully to avoid disturbing the plants. The tank will look best, and the filter will operate most efficiently, if it is filled almost to the top; in a plastic-framed aquarium, for instance, if the water level is above the bottom of the upper plastic trim of the aquarium but below the inner lip of the plastic frame.

Now you are ready to put on (or close) the cover, plug in the light, and start your filter—the subject of the next chapter.

Chapter Checkout

- You can check that the tank is level when you fill it to rinse out any dust.
- Wash the gravel and place it in the tank.
- Shape the gravel bed and add ornaments.
- Add real or plastic plants when the tank is one-third full.
- Fill the rest of the way and start the heater and filter.

Chapter 10

Starting and Operating the Filtration System

Once your tank is filled, it is time to start the filter. I can give you general instructions based on the way different types of filters operate, but there is enough individual variation among different models and brands that you have to read and follow the manufacturer's instructions for your particular filter.

What Lies Ahead

- setting up and maintaining your filter

PLUG AND PLAY

Two types of filters require merely installation and powering up. The undergravel filter is installed first in the aquarium, before the gravel is placed. After everything else, including the water, has been added, you either hook airlines to the lift tubes or set a powerhead on top of each tube. Then turn on the power (to the air pump or to the powerheads), and you're in business. The same is true for sponge filters, which are usually added to the tank at the end of setup but need only an air supply or a powerhead to begin functioning. (It is best to squeeze a sponge filter several times under water to displace the air inside the foam so it won't float.)

A MEDIA EVENT

All other types of filters need to be set up with media, and some require more elaborate preparations to begin operating. The basic medium in inside, outside, and canister filters is a mechanical medium—nylon pads, filter floss, sponge, fiber cartridges, etc. These media should be installed as per the manufacturer's instructions. When carbon is used, it should be placed in the appropriate compartment.

At this point, inside filters are simply placed into the aquarium and started, either by plugging them in (motorized filters) or by attaching them to an air line that has itself been connected to an air pump and then plugging in the air pump (air-operated filters). Outside power filters usually need to be started. Those that pump water from the aquarium into the filter will need to be primed with some water in the filter box.

Canister filters are more complicated, as they require positive seals at all connections. Make sure that you follow instructions, and be certain that all O-rings and clamps are tight. Many canister filters need to have a siphon started; the instruction will tell you the best way to do this.

GOING WITH THE FLOW

Once your filter is set up and started, you may need to adjust the flow. With a power filter or powerhead, the flow rate is often preset. With air-driven filters, you want a good, steady flow of air, which indicates a good, steady flow of water through the filter. If the flow is making the water "boil," you are getting very good aeration from all the surface turbulence.

With canister filters and with some power filters, you can adjust the direction and angle of the water return. For delicate fish and plants, a broad, gentle flow is best, while fast-water species prefer a real blast of water, such as they would get in a narrow stream. In any system, it is best to maximize the flow of water *across* the top of the water, since doing so maximizes gas exchange. When possible, adjust the water flow to be as horizontal as possible.

KEEPING THINGS CLEAN

The proper method of cleaning a filter depends on what the filter is supposed to be doing. Mechanical filters need regular and frequent replacement or cleaning of the filter media to remove the accumulated gunk and prevent it from contributing to the bioload. Remember, though, that any mechanical filter will also host a large number of beneficial biofiltration bacteria. You should minimize the destruction of these colonies if possible. If your filter has more than one compartment or filter pad, replace only one at a time; this will leave the bacteria in the other portions of the medium unharmed and will prevent a dangerous reduction in biofiltration capacity.

A chemical filtration medium doesn't need cleaning. If you are using carbon for either chemical filtration or biofiltration, it should be protected by a prefilter of mechanical medium to prevent it from becoming clogged with dirt. Should carbon being used for biofiltration get dirty, rinse it clean in a bucket of aquarium water. For chemical filtration, it should be replaced regularly. Unfortunately, there is no easy way to know when carbon's effectiveness has expired, so most hobbyists just change it on a regular basis; every four to six weeks is typical. There is no way you can recharge carbon at home. It can be done commercially in giant kilns, but the product is of reduced efficiency.

When the biofilter is also a mechanical filter, as with a sponge filter, the medium must be cleaned without destroying the biofilter. As I've mentioned before, the best way is to gently squeeze the sponge in a bucket of aquarium water to dislodge the dirt clogging the pores.

Canister filters are somewhat trickier in that they must be completely shut down, disconnected, and opened to clean the medium. This can be a messy and frustrating task if you do not have enough shutoffs in the plumbing, which is why I stressed that earlier in this book.

Variable Flow Rates

Some power filters have an adjustable flow rate, with a "feeding" setting. The idea is that by shutting the filter way down during feeding, you won't be sucking food into it before the fish eat it. Of course, if you follow the guidelines in this book, you will never be feeding so much food that that would happen anyway. Just remember that there is no such thing as too much filtration, and keep those filters going full blast.

MAINTAINING THE STATUS QUO

Gone are the days when aquarium filters needed regular oiling of the motor, adjustment of the impeller, and other servicing. Once established, a filtration system should continue to operate with just regular cleaning. You must be careful to observe its operation on a daily basis, however. Siphons can get plugged, lines can get pinched or disconnected, mechanical failures can occur. Filters with a power return will show a noticeable decrease in flow when the medium becomes plugged—something that regular cleaning will prevent and emergency cleaning will fix.

Do you ever have to tear the filter completely down? I'd love to be able to say no, but... Lots of things happen to a filter over time. Lime, algae, and crud can build up on the surfaces of

Follow the manufacture's instructions on how often you must replace filter media. Ignoring this may overload your biofilter.

parts; impellers wear down or out; and things can get out of alignment. A canister filter gets a miniature tear-down each time it is cleaned, but a power filter, especially one with custom fit cartridges, can go a long time between total break-downs. How long? Well, how long can a car go without a major repair? The same goes for filters—some will go on for years with no problems, others will need servicing long before that. I have several power filters that have been in continuous operation for more than ten years with no breakdown. Since most power filters have only one or two moving parts, mechanical failure is not common, and usually a new impeller is all that is needed. Often just a thorough cleaning of the entire filter will breathe new life into a deficient filter. It won't be necessary very often, however.

Annual Inspection

After a year of operation, tear down your filter and inspect the mechanisms. Use a brush to clean the tubing and other cavities, and check the impeller for excessive wear.

If there is little for you to do, next time wait a couple of years!

GET READY, SET...GO?

Okay, your filter is installed, the medium is in place, and you've started it. The water is flowing perfectly, and

Warning! Danger!

When the power goes out and a filter stops, so does the flow of water. Therefore the flow of oxygen also stops. This means that the biofilter bacteria are severely compromised. If the flow is stopped for an hour or more, you can count on considerable die-off, which may require a recycling of the tank. If the power is out for a long time, anaerobic conditions can permit the growth of dangerous bacteria in the filter. This is especially a problem with canister filters, which are not open to the air at all. When the power comes back on, poisons can be dumped into the tank. It is a good idea to disconnect a canister filter after a prolonged outage and discard the medium and the water in the filter. Since you probably won't be using a canister as your only biofilter, the overall loss should be minimal.

the system is ready to handle fish wastes. Or is it? Well, you're ready to start the tank cycling, but first let's take a quick breather and go over all the things you have to have coordinated before you even think of putting a fish into the tank.

Chapter Checkout

- Set up your filter per manufacturer's instructions with media of your choice.
- Cleaning filter media is a balance between removing accumulated crud and preserving biofiltration bacterial colonies.
- Most power filters can run a very long time without servicing other than regular cleaning.
- Once your filter is set up and running, it is time to start cycling the tank.

Chapter 11

Establishing Equilibrium

The best way to keep your fish healthy is to keep the conditions in the aquarium as stable as possible. This is true for many parameters, but especially those of water chemistry. The next chapter is devoted to that most important equilibrium, cycling, so here we'll look at other parameters that you want to keep stable.

What Lies Ahead

- keep things stable

TEMPERATURE REGULATION

Most tropical fish habitats experience differences in temperature that are more regional than seasonal. Still, shallow water tends to be very warm, while fast-flowing and deep waters tend to be cooler. In all, however, there is very little temperature variation in the tropical environment. The great rift lakes in Africa, for example, vary only a few degrees throughout the habitat.

Since fish are cold blooded, their metabolism depends on temperature, and at higher temperatures they grow, reproduce, and age more rapidly. They typically have such a narrow range of appropriate temperature, however, that there is not too great an effect within that range. Since keeping the temperature stable is more important than keeping it at a specific degree reading, the general rule of maintaining a temperature in the high 70s (24° to 26°C) is a good one.

When we talked about heaters, I explained their use in properly heating your aquarium water. But what about cooling it? During severe heat spells, you can make use of the cooling effect of evaporation to keep your tank from overheating. By positioning a fan blowing horizontally over the surface of the water, you will greatly increase evaporation, cooling the tank. Obviously you will have to keep adding water as you evaporate it from the tank.

If you have very hot summers, the best solution is to air condition the room in which the tank is situated. You can purchase an aquarium chiller, which uses refrigeration technology to cool the water to a set temperature, but often the chiller is more expensive than a room air conditioner and doesn't provide the side benefit of cooling you and your family.

No Cold Water

Do not make the mistake of trying to cool off your aquarium by adding cold water to it. The shock will do much more harm to your fish than the high temperature is likely to. Replacement water, however, can be a few degrees cooler than that in the aquarium. In cases of severe overheating, make several water changes, each one a couple of degrees cooler than the preceding. Never subject your fish to rapid changes in temperature.

LIGHT REGULATION

Since the tropics are characterized by year-round 12-hour days, tropical fish do not show the pronounced physiological reaction to day length that temperate or arctic species do. Many breeders maintain their fish under 24-hour lighting with no obvious ill effects.

The lighting period of your aquarium will, however, have a real effect on live plants. If you have a planted aquarium, it should receive about 10 to 12 hours of light per day for proper plant growth and health. Excessive light can increase growth rates, but it can also cause problems with algae.

PH DROP

Remember when I made you promise to do regular large water changes in exchange for not having to worry about water chemistry? And I said unless your water is extreme in pH, hardness, or alkalinity you could ignore chemistry completely? Well, in this discussion about equilibrium it is necessary to talk for a moment about pH drop, which can happen when the metabolic processes in your aquarium produce acids. If your water has little buffering capacity, properly called alkalinity, the acids can quickly drive down the pH, which means that the water gets more and more acidic. This is dangerous for your fish.

But we're going to assume your tap water does not have negligible alkalinity. Your aquarium retailer can probably tell you; just bring in a sample for testing. If you do have such extreme water, you will need to add a buffer every time you change the water, which, if anything, should be more often. But in almost all cases, pH drop will not be a concern in an aquarium that receives regular large water changes.

EVAPORATIVE CONCENTRATION

One of the things that causes water chemistry to change is evaporation. Since only water molecules evaporate, the dissolved materials—minerals, acids, bases, buffers, waste products—all stay behind. Thus as water continues to evaporate from the aquarium all of these substances become more concentrated.

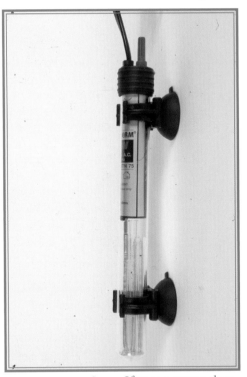

If you suspect that your heater is malfunctioning, unplug it first before reaching into your aquarium. Doing so prevents possible dangerous shocks.

The Four Seasons—Not

Temperate species tend to take seasonal cues from day length and temperature extremes. For example, many birds' reproductive cycles depend on the number of hours of light they receive each day, and many animals that hibernate will not breed if deprived of the hibernation cycle. Tropical species, such as many of our aquarium fish, however, often experience very little change in daylight or temperature over the course of a year. Typically, they do not have breeding seasons at all, but if they do, the seasons are usually correlated with flooding, since what characterizes tropical climates is alternating rainy and dry seasons. The implication for fish is that water chemistry is much more of a signal of the passage of time. Most aquarium species are not affected by day length or specific temperature, but they are very responsive to changes in water chemistry.

The most obvious effect of this is the buildup of "lime," or calcium deposits, on the glass at the water line and on glass tops above airlifts or filter returns, where splashing takes place. The deposits are primarily of only aesthetic concern, but they are reminders of the gradual increase in the hardness of the water as minerals become more concentrated.

Even more of a concern, however, is the unseen buildup of waste products, especially nitrate. Although most fish *can* adapt to very high nitrate concentrations if the change is gradual, they will do much better if it is not permitted to happen. Once again there is the problem that if these substances are allowed to accumulate, the fish will have been stressed initially by the buildup of wastes and the change in water chemistry, and then again when you do a water change by the addition of new water with vastly different (though improved) chemistry.

Some aquarists deal with these problems by using reverse osmosis water—water that is almost completely devoid of any dissolved materials—to top off evaporation. You probably will not find my personal solution surprising. I recommend *never* topping off evaporation, but instead doing water changes so often that evaporation does not become a concern. If there is a substantial lowering of the water level between water changes, just increase the frequency of the changes! This gives you the double advantage of not having to worry about evaporative concentration and what type of top-off water to use while at the same time giving your fish the healthiest environment possible. Remember that the goal is stability and equilibrium—if water doesn't stay in the tank very long, it won't have enough time to change chemically compared to the water from your tap.

Chapter Checkout

The best way to keep your fish healthy is to keep the conditions in the aquarium as stable as possible.

Temperature Stability

- Keeping the temperature stable is more important than keeping it at a specific degree reading.
- Maintain a temperature in the high 70s (24° to 26°C).
- Heaters protect against cool temperatures, but an aquarium should not be exposed to hot temperatures, either.

Light Regulation

- Most tropical species have little physiological reaction to light periods.
- Planted tanks should have a regular 10- to 12-hour photoperiod.

Chemical Stability

- If your water has little buffering capacity, properly called alkalinity, you will need to add a buffer every time you change the water, which, if anything, should be more often.
- In almost all other cases, chemical stability will not be a concern in an aquarium that receives regular large water changes.
- Do not top off evaporation. Change the water!

Chapter 12

Cycling—Behind the Mystique

Here we are finally—cycling your tank. In this practical, no-nonsense approach, you will learn all you need to know without the use of arcane rituals and secret formulas. Remember, what we're doing in the cycling operation is trying to get certain bacteria to grow so that they can be your biofilter. This is extremely important, but it isn't all that complicated. Since your biofiltration setup has already taken care of the oxygen and space requirements for the colonies, basically all you have to do now is feed them properly.

- how to cycle your aquarium

The proper food, of course, is ammonia—that horrible toxin! And as cycling progresses, that ammonia will be converted into still-toxic nitrite. Cycling, therefore, is a matter of balance between enough toxins to fuel the biofilter's growth and sufficiently low levels that your fish will survive. You can, however, get a mature biofilter without facing this challenge, and we will discuss this as well.

BETWEEN A ROCK AND A HARD PLACE

If you do not cycle your tank, your fish will die. But to feed the bacteria, you need to have fish in the tank to produce ammonia. How do you get out of this vicious circle? There are several ways, but an effective one is to use a few hardy fish to cycle the tank, then stock the rest of the fish slowly.

Nothing is harder for the new aquarist than to have a tank all set up with only two or three fish in it, but nothing is more important than to stock the tank slowly. The keys to proper tank cycling are patience, patience, and patience—and water testing.

When fish are added only a few at a time, the biofilter has sufficient time to build up additional colonies after each addition. The ammonia levels never rise too much, because the added wastes are kept to a minimum. Nevertheless, this is a stressful time for any fish in the tank, which is why we choose only the hardiest species as the first fish we put into the aquarium. Even so, losses can occur—another good reason to start with only a few fish.

Since you are starting out with a negligible number of bacteria in the setup, the ammonia produced by the fish simply dissolves in the water. After a period of time, the first set of bacteria will be established, and they will consume the ammonia and produce nitrite. The nitrite will now accumulate until the second batch of bacteria become established. Then they will consume the nitrite and produce nitrate. You can see, therefore, that the cycling of your aquarium can be tracked by testing the water.

At first ammonia will begin to concentrate. A while later, the ammonia concentration will gradually drop to zero while nitrite will begin to increase. Still later, the nitrite will go to zero as nitrate accumulates. You can follow this process with your test kits.

You must realize that there are many variables affecting the length of time it takes for the bacterial colonies to grow to effective sizes. Temperature, water chemistry, the type and

The Cycling Dilemma

No, the cycling dilemma isn't about the decision whether to wear cotton or polyester for that 50-mile ride. It's about getting the biofilter started in your aquarium, and it's the most important thing you can learn from this book.

To cycle your tank, the bacteria in the biofilter must be fed, which means you need a source of ammonia in the aquarium on which the bacteria can feed—typically some fish. Until the bacterial colonies are established, however, ammonia can build up in the tank to dangerous levels, putting great stress on any fish in there. While there is no perfect answer, there are various solutions to this problem, and you can take your pick of them in this chapter on tank cycling.

number of fish, what you feed them, and even the species of bacteria in your tank all contribute. It is a very good idea to "jump start" the cycling by adding a handful of gravel from an established aquarium, or even some dirty filter medium from a healthy aquarium. This introduces cycling bacteria, giving your biofilter a head start over waiting for the right bacterial spores to land in your tank. However, even if you do nothing other than fill the tank with water from the tap, the bacteria will eventually establish themselves.

Cycle That Tank!

There is no substitute for cycling. Without a mature biofilter, your tank will fail, period.

A STRAIGHTFORWARD PROTOCOL FOR SUCCESS

Nowhere is the advice to take it easy more useful than in cycling your aquarium. By starting slowly, by stocking gradually, by stalling the process whenever waste production starts to get ahead of bacterial growth, you can have a successful first tank and avoid the ranks of aquarists who give up. Let's look at methods of growing a mature biofilter. We'll first consider the traditional method, using a few fish to provide the necessary ammonia, and then look at some less stressful methods.

Pushing the Nitrogen Limit

As a general rule, you want the values for the three N's (ammonia, nitrite, nitrate) to be as low as possible (preferably zero), but the nature of tank cycling means that the concentrations of ammonia and then nitrite *must* climb disturbingly high in order to provide the food for the initial bacterial growth. Your test kits will come with detailed instructions and charts (usually color-coded) that indicate which values are considered negligible, moderate, dangerous, and extremely dangerous.

There are several variables that determine how high is "too" high. Since different species, and even different individuals of a given species, have varying tolerances to ammonia and nitrites, it is impossible to give exact values at which you should do a water change. Of course, if you get a reading in the danger zone you must quickly change some water, but make sure you also observe your fish for signs of stress. Gasping at the surface is an obvious one you hope to avoid, but rapid breathing and unusually skittish behavior are also signs of levels too high for the fish. The levels can be too high for your fish without going into the danger zone, so be prepared to err on the side of caution. The worst result will be a slight lengthening in the cycling process, but not intervening at the appearance of signs of fish distress can result in loss of the fish.

Patience, Patience, Patience

The first thing you need to cycle your tank is *patience;* cycling cannot be rushed. It is difficult to be in such a passive role, but you must wait for the biofilter to come up to full speed. Once you muster the patience, however, the task is very straightforward:

Step 1: Put a few hardy fish into the tank. Do not feed them.

Step 2: The next day, check the ammonia level.

a. If it is above safe bounds, do a 30- to 50-percent water change, then check the ammonia. If it is still too high, do another water change. Go back to Step 2 the following day.

b. Even if ammonia is within the safety range, do not feed. Go to Step 3.

Step 3: The next day, check the ammonia level.

a. If it is above safe bounds, do a 30- to 50-percent water change, then check the ammonia. If it is still too high, do another water change. Return to Step 3 the following day.

b. If it is within safe limits, you may feed an infinitesimal amount of food—barely visible. Go to Step 4 the following day.

Step 4: Check the ammonia level.

a. If it is above safe bounds, do a 30- to 50-percent water change, then check the ammonia. If it is still too high, do another water change. Return to Step 4 the following day.

b. If ammonia is within safe bounds and the fish are not stressed, feed a minimal amount. Return to Step 4 until nitrite begins to accumulate. Then go to Step 5.

Step 5: Continue cycling.

As a general rule after a too-high reading, continue to monitor without feeding until the ammonia or nitrite remains at safe levels for three days. The fish will not starve, and there will be plenty of ammonia or nitrite being produced without their being fed. Once the tests have been within safe bounds without a water change for three days, feed them very lightly once a day and continue testing the water daily.

Next you should see nitrite begin to appear and ammonia decline. Once again, if the nitrite climbs into the danger zone, do a 30- to 50-percent water change, even more if necessary. Finally nitrite will drop as nitrate begins to accumulate.

Once nitrite has peaked and begun to fall and nitrate has begun to accumulate, you're almost home! When both ammonia and nitrite remain at zero, your tank has cycled. You can now add fish gradually, a few at a time. Always feed lightly and test the water daily after an addition. If or when the values remain at zero for ammonia and nitrite after a few days, you can continue to add fish until the tank is fully stocked. If you get a spike of ammonia or nitrite, it's time to pull out your patience again and wait for this minicycle to finish before adding any additional fish.

What if All Your Fish Are Wimps?

What happens if none of the fish you plan to keep are really tough enough to withstand the rigors of cycling? Well, there are several ways to deal with this problem without getting too complicated.

A Note About Water Testing

Hopefully you will rarely or never get a reading that goes into the danger zone. If, however, you get a test result that comes out at the top of the scale for that test, you won't know the actual value. For example, if your ammonia test kit can test up to 10 ppm, and you get the maximum reading, there is no way to know whether the actual value is 10 or 1000. You can determine the true value by the dilution method, but since maximum readings are extremely bad news no matter what, it is much more important to get the reading down with massive water changes than to figure out its exact value. Just remember to test again after the water change. In the event that the uppermost reading was caused by a phenomenally massive concentration of ammonia, it is possible that a single water change will leave the tank still in the danger zone. Do not assume the water is safe without re-testing. Repeat the test after each water change, and keep doing water changes until the tests are okay.

SLOW STOCKING

When at least one of the species you've selected is fairly hardy, you can use a more gradual stocking. You still need to monitor the water parameters with your test kits, but instead of putting a few fish in to cycle the tank before adding any others, you start with one fish and gradually add more, maybe one per week. This makes cycling take longer because of the very gradual increase in available food for the bacteria, but it also minimizes the dangerous peaks in ammonia and nitrite that fuel a more rapid bacterial growth.

Since you're going to have a medium to large aquarium, it will be large enough to provide a lot of dilution for fish wastes, so you can use gradual stocking with all but the most sensitive species, though you would want to use *extremely* gradual stocking, perhaps one fish every ten to fourteen days. That's an acceptable way of doing it, but it means an awful lot of trips back and forth to the pet shop for one little fish. You also have to be ready to do a water change at the first sign of ammonia or nitrite buildup; that will slow cycling down even more, but it will protect your fish.

SWITCHING SPECIES

Another way of cycling a tank for non-hardy fish is to use a different species of fish to cycle it, then remove it and stock the desired species. In this case you are setting up only the one aquarium, so you will have to borrow some fish from a friend, or else discuss the matter with your dealer—perhaps you can purchase a group of fish and return them after the cycling. Maybe you'll even be able to exchange them for credit toward the other fish you want.

Recommended species are guppies and platies among the livebearers, with zebra danios, white clouds, and rosy barbs among the egglayers. Some people recommend using goldfish, but that is advisable only if you are not using feeder goldfish, which could easily contaminate your tank with parasites and diseases. It is often difficult, however, to find hardy non-fancy goldfish that are *not* feeders—you want comets or common goldfish, or perhaps fantails, since the fancier varieties are more delicate. Some cichlids are hardy enough to cycle a tank, and it is usually not too difficult to find some convict cichlids for free or very cheaply because they are so prolific. The problem will be in finding someone to take them after you're done!

If you build up a normal population of fish in the tank, then remove all the fish and immediately replace them with a different set of fish, your biofilter should continue unaffected. Whenever you make any changes to a tank, however, you should monitor the water for a few days to make sure there is no ammonia spike.

Isn't There an Easier Way?

Can you avoid the trouble of cycling your tank? Yes! Even though people speak about cycling an aquarium, what you are really doing is establishing a biofilter. So if you can establish a biofilter some other way, your tank will not need cycling.

I myself almost never cycle a tank. Cycling is immensely important, but it isn't something I want to use my valuable fish for, so I cheat. There are two methods I use for providing my newly set up tanks with a mature biofilter.

Too Much Wastes

Mythconception: Many hobbyists feel that water changes during cycling are a very bad idea. They argue that you're removing the ammonia or nitrite upon which the new bacterial colonies must feed.

Reality: The reason levels rise too high is that there are not enough bacteria eating the wastes. If you do not do a water change, the fish will suffer (or die) during the time the bacterial colonies are building up. Without the water changes, you will be subjecting your fish to intolerable conditions just so that you can be done with the cycling a week sooner. Cycling can take up to a couple of months, though it is usually finished in less than half that time. Patience.

Glass catfish should not be used to cycle a new aquarium. They can be extremely sensitive to fluctuating water chemistry.

SMOKE AND MIRRORS

There is no way you can get around the necessity of maturing a biofilter for your tank, but there is a way you can make it *look* as if you did. What you are actually doing is letting a mature aquarium system culture your biofilter for you, then placing it already mature into your new tank.

Here's the recipe for no-cycle cycling. The crucial ingredient is a friend, neighbor, acquaintance, relative, or friendly aquarium dealer who is willing to help you with this recipe. If they agree to help, you're all set!

- Buy two big sponge filters. They will be in addition to any other filter(s) you have decided to use on your tank.
- Set them up in a tank full of high ammonia producers—a bustling cichlid tank is a great choice, but your helper will know which tank to use.
- Leave the filters running in your helper's tank for six weeks.
- In the meantime, set up your aquarium with everything but the fish. Since you are going to use filters other than

How To Handle the Not-So-Hardy

The fish I want in my tank are not hardy species recommended for cycling. What do I do?

Best Choice: Use different fish for cycling and put in the desired species once the biofilter is established.

Acceptable Alternative: Use extremely gradual stocking, starting with one or two fish and adding them one or two more at a time at intervals of a week or so.

the two sponge filters on a permanent basis, get them running too.

At the end of six weeks, buy half of the fish for your tank. On your way home, stop and get the two sponge filters from your helper. Keep them wet, but do not transport them submersed in water! You want a wet-dry situation—taken from the tank and put into a plastic bag with just the water in the sponge is fine. Hurry home and place the filters into your tank and start them, then start acclimating your fish and put them into the tank.

The next morning, test your water for ammonia and nitrite. If there are any, do a water change, but I'm betting there won't be any. If the next morning there still aren't any, go get the rest of your fish.

You have to monitor your water every day for a while to make sure that there is no ammonia spiking, but there probably won't be.

If you plan on discontinuing the sponge filters, wait a few weeks and then remove one of them. Monitor your water for any problems. If there are none, wait a few more weeks and remove the other one. By then your permanent filtration system will have matured; test the water for a few days to make sure, and always be ready to do a water change if you get a spike of ammonia or nitrite.

STEALING A BIOFILTER

A related way of getting instant cycling is to steal another tank's biofilter. If you are careful, you can do this without dooming the other tank. The first requirement is that both your new tank and this other tank are using the same make and model of biofiltration equipment, making the media completely interchangeable. For instance, I use the same type of filter on all of my tanks so that I can move the biomedia around, and when setting up a new tank I routinely use half of the biofiltration media of one of my existing filters in the filter of the new tank. This of course leaves the existing tank with only half of its biofiltration capacity, so I have to be careful and monitor that tank for a few days to make sure that it has adequate biofiltration. But it also gives the new tank half a functioning biofilter, which is sufficient if I don't stock that tank fully right away. Obviously, this method is not an option if the established tank is densely stocked and on the verge of being overcrowded.

HALFWAY MEASURES

Both of these methods of maturing a biofilter outside your new tank require, of course, that you have access to a mature aquarium, and they don't save any steps or work, but they do save a lot of worry and hassle in the close monitoring needed when cycling a tank from scratch. They also leave the original tank at some risk, especially in the second method, but the fact that the remaining biofiltration is perfectly mature usually means that any minicycling of the tank from which the biomedium is removed is rapid and uneventful.

There are, however, other things you can do to speed up cycling. I've already mentioned taking some dirty filter medium or some gravel from an established healthy aquarium to

Instant Cycling?

In my active fish breeding room, I often need to set up a tank on almost no notice. How do I handle cycling in these instances? Easy—I cheat!

As I've mentioned, I love oscars and typically have several tanks of these big food-hogging ammonia producers. I usually keep a whole line of sponge filters bubbling away in these tanks along with the regular filters. These filters do give some additional biofiltration, which is very welcome in these tanks, but their purpose is to be available when I set up a new tank. I simply take one of these mature biofilters out of the oscar tank and plop it into the new tank—instant cycling! Then I put a new filter into the oscar tank, where it becomes last in line, but it will be mature by the time all the others are taken ahead of it. If you can mature a biofilter in another tank, it can serve as an instant biofilter for your new tank.

"seed" the bacteria in your new tank. These things can be done a little more aggressively, too.

For example, if you know someone who is *not* using an undergravel (UGF) as a biofilter, you can take all of the gravel from that person's tank without diminishing its biofiltration much at all, but it will give your new tank a real boost, since even without a UGF a gravel bed holds a lot of biofiltration bacteria. Someone with a planted tank would not be interested in swapping new gravel for old, but many aquarists with fish-only setups would be willing to do this. A variant of this is to take rocks, driftwood, or ornaments from an established tank. Again, you may be able to find an aquarist willing to let you purchase a new ornament in exchange for the old one bearing beneficial bacteria colonies.

These methods will *not* provide instant cycling, but they will decrease the time it takes to cycle your tank. In some cases this decrease can be dramatic; in others it is barely noticeable—chalk it up to the vagaries of culturing bacteria.

Fishless Cycling

In recent years "fishless cycling" has gained many proponents. These methods all use something other than live fish as an ammonia source. The benefit of these methods is that you aren't risking the welfare of any of your fish, and without animals in the tank you can allow ammonia levels to rise into the danger zone, which can speed up cycling considerably.

Some people use a hunk of fish meat or shellfish, partially burying it in the gravel. As the meat rots, it produces ammonia. An alternative is to use fish food, adding a pinch each day to decompose and produce ammonia. You can also avoid rotting altogether and add ammonium chloride or ammonium hydroxide directly to the aquarium, providing instant food for the biofiltration bacteria.

With any of these methods, you still need to test to follow the progress, but there is no urgency, and you can allow the levels to rise much higher before doing a water change.

On the Horizon

No discussion of tank cycling would be complete without mentioning a new technology that promises 24-hour cycling of any aquarium. It is based on the use of large amounts of a special highly activated carbon as the biomedium, extremely high water flows, and a proprietary blend of a large number of bacterial strains. This technology comes from waste water management, where it has been successfully used in some extremely difficult sewage treatment situations. As these products are tested in aquarists' tanks and gain acceptance over the course of time, there is a good chance that they will become available through local retailers. Already on the market are some proprietary live bacteria cultures supposedly useful in speeding up the cycling process. As is the case with most other products, some work and some don't. Check with your aquarium store personnel.

But note that this technology does not do away with cycling. It simply uses bacteria that have extremely rapid growth rates to establish a mature biofilter in a matter of hours instead of days or weeks. If preliminary tests indicate the normal performance of these products, they will cause a revolution in aquarium maintenance, and they will help reduce the failure-based attrition among new hobbyists. Keep an eye out for this and other technology as the new millennium brings more and more wonders to our venerable hobby.

Chapter Checkout

Cycling is critical for the survival of your fish, but it is not very complicated.
* It is a matter of balancing having the toxins needed to fuel bacterial growth without harming the fish.
* There are, however methods of establishing a biofilter that do not require you to expose live fish to the rigors of cycling.

Basic cycling:
* Patience is required.
* Gradual stocking of the aquarium with hardy fish.
    * The slower you stock, the longer cycling takes, but the easier it is on the fish.
    * You can cycle with hardy species and then replace them with the desired fish.
* Testing.
    * You must test the water daily for ammonia and nitrite.
    * If either is too high, do a water change to bring the level down.
* A regular progression.

Some hobbyists cycle their tanks with fish and some do not. The choice is yours.

- You will start with zero levels for ammonia, nitrite, and nitrate.
- Ammonia will rise first.
- Then nitrite will begin to accumulate, and ammonia will decrease.
- When nitrite peaks, nitrate will accumulate.
- When ammonia and nitrite remain at zero, the job is done.

An easier way:
- Use a biofilter matured in another tank.
- Share the biomedium from a mature filter with the new tank.
- Take some bacteria from a mature tank.
  - gravel
  - plants
  - decorations
  - dirty filter medium
- Add a product containing live bacteria.

Fishless Cycling
  - A hunk of fish or shellfish rots to produce ammonia.
  - Ammonia is added chemically, as ammonium chloride or hydroxide.

Products using rapidly reproducing biofiltration bacteria hold promise for the future.

Chapter *13*

Regular Maintenance

One of the nice things about maintaining an aquarium is that it is not very difficult or time consuming. One of the bad things is that it is not always immediately apparent if you are negligent in your responsibilities, unlike a dirty cat litter box or an unwashed dog, both of which send out powerful olfactory reminders. If you neglect your aquarium's care you will see a gradual deterioration in the fish's health; if the neglect is prolonged, all your fish will get sick and die. The extreme hardiness of most tropical fish can work to their disadvantage when you allow their capacity to adapt to poor conditions to delay your routine maintenance chores.

- regular maintenance
- feeding protocol
- prevention and quarantine

Many of the topics in this chapter have been touched on throughout the book. What we're doing here is bringing them all together and integrating them into a more detailed regimen of regular aquarium care.

DAILY QUICK CHECK

You should get into the habit of checking on your setup every day—in fact, every time you look at it. Some things tend to get noticed right away, like the family cat thrashing frantically in the tank, or water on the carpet under it. Very often, however, much less obvious problems need just as immediate attention.

A quick look-over can allow you to keep track of many things. Is the temperature correct? Is the filter running? Do the fish appear stressed—gasping at the surface, hiding in the corners, lying on the bottom? Is the water cloudy? Are there unusual or unpleasant odors? When you feed your fish, notice their behavior. Do they respond normally, or do they seem listless?

Many serious problems can be averted by simply checking to see whether things look normal and that all the equipment is functioning. For example, a filter's functioning can be stopped by many things—a blocked intake tube, an electrical disconnection, plugged filter media, or something else. Left unnoticed and uncorrected, this can lead to wholesale disaster, but if caught right away, such things are easily fixed. Combine your vigilance with faithful performance of routine maintenance chores and you will avoid almost all serious situations.

REGULAR CHORES

General cleaning should be performed in conjunction with water changes, which means no less often than weekly. In fact, if you perform daily water changes and vacuumings you may hardly ever have to clean your filter.

Check This Checklist

Checking your aquarium daily is the best way to prevent serious problems from developing. You should check:
- temperature
- condition of fish (and plants)
- appearance of water
- operation of filter
- overall status quo

Cleaning the Filter

Although this comes first to mind for many people, cleaning the aquarium filter is not an overwhelming priority. This is because the primary function of the filter is biofiltration, which actually is optimal when the filter is left undisturbed. On the other hand, the material trapped in the filter continues to decompose even though it is not floating around the aquarium. That is why a filter with a separate biomedium is a great idea; the mechanical filter medium, which traps suspended dirt, can be cleaned regularly, removing this material from the tank's water circulation, while the biomedium can be left undisturbed.

Cleaning your tank will keep your fish healthy, happy, and beautiful. Pictured is a fancy guppy, *Poecilia reticulata*.

The mechanical filtration medium also keeps the biomedium from becoming plugged with particles, permitting it a full flow of water to keep the bacterial colonies healthy. Aquariums in which an undergravel filter serves as the biomedium must have the gravel vacuumed regularly, as already described.

A rotating contactor filter is designed this way, with the wheel on which the bacterial colonies grow being fed with water that has already passed through a mechanical filter medium or media. Many filters contain a series of chambers through which the water flows; if the biofilter medium is located in the last chamber, the water reaching it will also have been filtered of all suspended material. Clean the filter medium weekly, but leave the biomedium alone unless it becomes plugged (which it won't if you keep the rest of the filter cleaned). When you clean the mechanical medium, wash it in a bucket of aquarium water, not chlorinated tap water, since even the mechanical filtration medium you clean regularly will support a lot of bacterial colonies.

Vacuuming the Bottom

In the same way, siphoning detritus off the bottom of the tank removes sources of decomposition (while improving the aesthetics), which decreases the bioload of the tank. This is easily done as part of the routine water changes, using a siphon with a gravel tube attachment. This simple device relies on basic fluid dynamics to decrease the suction so that the gravel is lifted and separated but not drawn into the hose, while the dirt trapped in it is liberated and sucked out into the hose.

Water Changes

Regular partial water changes are the most important maintenance procedure you can perform. Regular large water changes can eliminate the need for a great deal of equipment, testing, and treatment. They do more to help maintain a beneficial environment for your fish than any other aspect of aquarium husbandry. Water changes can prevent or reduce most fish diseases and make your fish healthier, happier, and more colorful. Regular water changes have no unpleasant side effects. It is not surprising, therefore, that I have been stressing regular large water changes as the most crucial aspect of succeeding with your first aquarium.

How Much? How Often?

Unless you live in an area where water use must be restricted, where water might be too expensive a commodity to be used freely in the first place, the only limit on how much water you change and how often you do it is your willingness to perform the task.

No amount of filtration can make up for a deficiency in water changes, but water changes can make up for deficiencies in filtration. If you change water often enough you won't need any filtration at all. Yet even I—water-changing fanatic that I am—recognize that such systems are practical for maybe only one hobbyist out of a thousand, and almost never for beginning hobbyists.

The easiest way to become a successful aquarist is to consider your filtration system to be an aid you use to keep the water clean between water changes. You should remove and replace a minimum of half of the water every week. If you follow this regimen faithfully, you will maintain a high level of water quality. This is an acceptable level of water change, and—even combined with the task of cleaning the filter medium as needed—it doesn't really add up to a lot of work.

It would be wonderful, however, if you could manage an even greater rate of change. Your fish will truly thrive on such a regimen.

Performing a water change is a simple matter of draining off some water and replacing it with fresh. Removing the water requires a siphon hose with gravel tube and a bucket. You don't even need the bucket if your siphon reaches a drain (or out the window if you're lucky enough to be in a situation that lets you get away with such a maneuver).

Start the siphon and work your way around the aquarium, gently inserting the end of the gravel tube into the gravel. The grains of gravel will rise partway up, and you will see the dirt being sucked out as they fall back down. When sufficient water has been removed, it is time to refill. And just as you don't even need the bucket if you have a drain, you don't even need a gravel tube if you don't have gravel in the tank—but you do have to be more careful about what the siphon sucks out.

Vacuuming your substrate sucks up fish waste, rotting food, and breaks up anaerobic (without oxygen) spots that can lead to harmful bacterial growth.

Refilling can be done by bucket or hose. There are two very important things to remember about the replacement water—it must be dechlorinated if necessary, and it must be at the same temperature as the aquarium water. Fish can withstand a slight difference in temperature, but make sure the water is within a degree or two of the aquarium temperature.

If you use a bucket to refill the tank, you can add the dechlorinator in the bucket. With a hose, it is best to add it before you refill the tank. The current from the hose will keep the water well mixed, and the dechlorinator in the water will react with the chlorine/chloramine as it arrives.

You can see that most of the "work" involved in changing the water is in getting out the hose and buckets and putting them away. It is not that much more difficult to change half the water instead of only a quarter, and the added benefits of the larger changes make it well worth the effort. I know that you're going to take what I say here with a grain of salt because you know by now that I'm a water-changing fanatic. But I'm realistic enough to know that each aquarist is different and that you might not be able to follow as strict a schedule as I do, but remember that if you stray too far off the prescribed track you're unquestionably going to start running

Cleaning Sponge Filters

A biofilter should be cleaned rarely, if ever. The exception to this is a sponge filter, which doubles as a mechanical filter. The sponge should be cleaned regularly by squeezing it gently in a bucket of aquarium water. The idea is to clear the pores so water can flow freely without dislodging the bacterial colonies in the sponge.

into trouble with your aquarium. Do yourself and your fish a favor by doing the one thing that will guarantee a successful beginning—and a very rewarding long life—to your career as an aquarium hobbyist: make those needed water changes.

DEGASSING

We cannot leave the topic of water changes without touching on the concept of degassing. You already know that as temperature increases water can hold less and less by way of dissolved gases. If your water supply is cold, especially in the winter, it can contain a great deal of dissolved air. You may also be aware that more gas can dissolve in water when it is under pressure. When cold water is heated in a pressurized system like your household plumbing and water heater, the gas cannot escape—until you put it into your aquarium.

When you open a bottle of carbonated beverage, the release of pressure permits the carbonation (dissolved carbon dioxide) to bubble out of solution. The same thing happens on a smaller scale when you fill your aquarium. The phenomenon often produces a film of tiny bubbles all over the aquarium, the decorations, and even the fish. This is *extremely dangerous*! The dissolved gases can enter the fish's bloodstream through the gills, but after a short time the gases will bubble out of solution within the fish's bodies, causing embolisms—gas bubbles that can cripple or kill a fish. In the same way that a scuba diver rising too quickly from the depths can suffer the bends, fish with high dissolved gas levels in their blood will suffer injury or death.

Fortunately, there is an easy fix to this problem. While it takes a few minutes for the gas to bubble out of solution when exposed to regular air pressure, it escapes very quickly if the water is vigorously agitated. In most cases using a nozzle on the hose with which you fill the aquarium (or the bucket used to fill the aquarium) and aiming a strong jet of water against the side of the container will cause sufficient turbulence to drive off the extra dissolved gases. You want the water to "boil" with bubbles and agitation. The bubbles, of course, are from air mixing with the water at the

Tiny bubbles in your tank after a water change indicate gas supersaturation, which has the potential to casue serious harm to your fish.

surface, but the agitation they produce is what releases the dissolved gases. If you ever see tiny bubbles in your aquarium after a water change, you have not degassed the water vigorously enough.

"Waste" Water

Many people are rightly concerned with water conservation, and they might balk at an aggressive water change regimen. Remember, however, how little water even extreme water changes require compared to typical household usage. (See Chapter 7.)

Also keep in mind the uses to which this water can be put. During gardening months, you would probably want to drain the tank into the garden, or into a barrel in the garden, from which you can scoop water for irrigation purposes. Do you have livestock? Aquarium water is normally fine for other animals to drink. In fact, our cats leave their water bowls untouched and always drink from our aquariums—they must like the fishy taste! It's a simple matter to drain aquarium waste water into stock tanks, which again means that your water changes are actually saving water by making it do double duty.

Okay, okay, you live in an apartment, not in a house, and certainly not on a farm, so none of this drain-your-water-into-a-barrel-and-give-it-to-the-horses stuff is very exciting for you. But it still applies, even if only on a smaller scale. And maybe you'll keep it in mind for the day you move into more bucolic surroundings.

Underfeeding

Feeding is certainly the most regular of regular maintenance procedures. I've labeled this section "underfeeding" to emphasize that you must avoid overfeeding. While it is true that some fish will gorge themselves until they become sick, the major problem with overfeeding is that the tank becomes polluted by both the rotting of uneaten food and the increased metabolic wastes from the overfed fish. In hobbyists' tanks, obese fish with fatty liver disease are quite common, but emaciated, starving fish are not. We all tend to be too generous with our pets, who are adapted to a world where meals do not come with any particular regularity.

Many fish food containers and many aquarium books have rules of thumb for feeding your fish such *as much as they can eat in five minutes.* Unfortunately, it takes a while before you have enough experience to know how much they'll eat in any given time span, so here is a specific four-part guide for feeding your fish. You should follow it very closely until such time as you feel confident in recognizing and understanding from your fish's behavior when they have had enough to eat. I guarantee you that whatever amount you think you should feed, it is too much—probably *way* too much. I'm going to repeat that for emphasis: I guarantee you that whatever amount you think you should feed, it is too much—probably *way* too much.

Here are the four steps to learning how to feed fish:

Examine their eyes and mouths. Look at your fish. Focus on their eyes and their mouths. Most aquarium fish are tiny. They have tiny mouths and eyes—their stomachs are about the size of their eyes! You're not feeding kittens or puppies here, and the amounts of food you need are relatively very small.

Count the flakes. Count your fish. Let's say there are 22 of them. Now take a container of flake food and count out—actually count out on a piece of paper on a table—22 flakes. Now compare the flake size to the fish's mouth size. Many of the flakes will be two or three mouthfuls at least.

Watch as you feed. Now drop those flakes into the tank. Observe your fish. Do they all get something to eat? If so, you've fed your fish. You should come back and repeat the process later in the day. No, you don't have to count out flakes before each feeding; after a few times, you will be able to judge a "pinch" of food that is the right size.

If some of the fish got nothing to eat, was it because one or two bullies hogged all the food, or was it because there wasn't enough to go around? You may have to drop the food into different spots in the tank to let them all get their share.

Do the fish seem less hungry after eating this much food? Are any of them visibly plumper? You do not want your fish to swell up like balloons—which most will if you overfeed them, but it is usually easy to see if they have filled their bellies. A slight complication here arises from the fact that females of both egglaying and livebearing species can get to look very round-bellied

What's "Normal" Behavior?

In order to discern unusual behavior, you need to know what normal behavior is. For the vast majority of fish, lying motionless on the bottom is not normal, but there are several species for which it is, and one popular fish—the clown loach—will even lie on its side, giving its naive keeper a real scare.

Most fish keep their fins fully extended when they are feeling well, but a healthy male betta will often close his extra-long fins whenever he isn't swimming or displaying to a rival—while also lying on the bottom!

Pale colors on a fish are usually a danger sign, but not right after you put on the lights, since most fish go pale at night. That practical-joking clown loach also goes pale when in a dominance struggle—a time most other species get more intense colors.

Likewise, a fish that has turned dark is often a very sick fish. Many cichlids, however, darken when spawning, and some turn completely black.

White spots or bumps are almost always a cause for extreme concern, but among many (especially non-tropical) cyprinid species—goldfish, for example—white spots on the head and gill covers of male fish indicate breeding readiness.

Once again, the key to success is knowledge.

as they become filled with eggs or their babies develop—but as you gain experience you'll be able to make the distinction between overfeeding and reproduction easily enough.

Do your nocturnal fish come out to feed? (Many will; some won't.) If not, their food will have to be put in after lights out.

Wait. As the days go by, you will be better and better able to judge the correct amount to feed your fish, given their nature and your schedule. If you can feed them only once or twice a day, obviously they will need more per feeding than if you are home and can feed them tiny portions five times a day. These guidelines will keep you from overfeeding your fish while it keeps them from getting too hungry, which gives you time to learn. This is the correct way, the *successful* way, to learn to feed your fish, one much preferable to the common scenario of someone learning the dangers of overfeeding by losing an entire tankful of fish. It will protect them from premature death, and it will set you on the way to having a long-term successful aquarium.

A Wet Green Thumb?

Do you garden? Then think of your aquarium as a reservoir for plant water! Passing water through your tank before you water your plants not only gets double service from the same water but also improves your fish's health while taking care of your plants!

STARVATION

Starvation may seem a strange topic to include, but it is important for you to understand some fundamental characteristics of cold-blooded fish. Although their frenzied delight when you feed them will reinforce the notion that fish view eating with the same feelings and emotions as a dog or a cat or you or I, the fact is that fish do not suffer from food deprivation until long after a warm-blooded animal would be severely weakened or dead. A small rodent deprived of food for 24 hours is likely to starve to death, while a much smaller fish can easily experience a two-week fast without injury.

In fact, an occasional period without feeding can be beneficial. You do not have to schedule regular fast days into your maintenance program (though many aquarists do, especially hobbyists who keep large predatory fishes), but you can skip a feeding now and then, and you certainly should *not* have someone come in and feed your fish if you are going to be away two weeks or less. It is much healthier for your pets to go unfed than to be subject to the well-motivated but lethal ministrations of an otherwise well-meaning overfeeder.

Are Periodic Breakdowns Necessary?

It is my personal experience that tanks get dismantled most often because they are being moved to a new location or re-outfitted for a different batch of fish. Since you're tearing them down anyway, you wash the gravel thoroughly, scrape all the glass clean, etc. Barring such renovations, however, a well-managed aquarium does not need to be overhauled like that. The *if it ain't broke, don't fix it* adage applies here.

Won't My Fish Stop Eating When They Are Full?

Fish are always looking for food. Their physiology and behavior have been adapted to a constant hunting mode. In the wild, food isn't delivered three times a day by a strange biped holding portions of food. It's very much catch-as-catch-can in the world of fish, so fish do not have well-developed mechanisms to stop feeding, and most will become grotesquely bloated before they actually refuse food. Don't kill your fish with kindness—feed them all they need, not all they will take!

New aquarists, however, sometimes wind up with a real mess of a tank, and it is important to realize that you *can* start over. Often when all of someone's fish die, that person gives up, but some want to try again. If their tank is a cesspool, putting new fish into it is unlikely to be any more successful than the last batch was. What were those newbie pitfalls? New Tank Syndrome—improper cycling, overfeeding, and overcrowding. What characterizes all of them? Lack of beneficial bacteria and overabundance of putrefactive bacteria. What's the cure? Tank breakdown and cleaning.

FIXING THINGS UP

If your tank crashes and goes septic, a total cleaning is in order. You will probably find that the gravel is stained black and smells like rotten eggs. That's hydrogen sulfide. The bacteria (and stench) can be washed out, but the gravel may remain stained. In cases like this, or when a virulent disease has wiped out your fish and you are afraid it may still be lurking in the tank, you may want to sterilize the system. Let's hope you never need this information, but if you do, here it is.

This extreme procedure can save aquarium equipment that would otherwise be unsafe to use. However, no cleaner, soap, or detergent is safe to use on an aquarium or on anything that goes into it—except for bleach. The active ingredient in household bleach is sodium hypochlorite, usually called "chlorine." This and related chemicals are used in municipal water disinfection and in swimming pools. It is an unstable substance that breaks down with time, heat, and aeration, and it is easily neutralized with sodium thiosulphate, the substance in all dechlorinators.

You can therefore bleach an aquarium, its gravel, and its ornaments as long as you are very careful to eliminate all the residual bleach before you add any fish. Rinsing the tank several times and letting it dry should be sufficient, but remember that you have to get *all* of it out. Gravel and ornaments that can stand it can be rinsed in boiling or very hot water, which should eliminate the hypochlorite.

If you can still smell "chlorine," you have more work to do. Once the odor is gone, you can use a test kit to check for residual chlorine, but an easier way is to fill the tank with all the decorations in it, then treat with a megadose of aquarium dechlorinator—maybe 10 times the normal dose. Then drain the tank and refill once or twice or until there no longer is any smell.

HEALTH CARE

As I said earlier, you aren't going to be running a medical diagnostic lab or using a spectrum of medications. In fact, almost all health issues are answered with preventive measures. The first part of disease prevention is stress elimination, and the first place your fish will get stressed is when you bring them home. They have already been stressed plenty before they are netted by your dealer to put into a bag for you. So let's see how to make the transition to your tank as stress-free as possible.

Introducing Your Fish

No, this section isn't about "How do you do, swordtail? May I present catfish." It's about the proper way to acclimate your fish and to introduce them into their new home—your aquarium.

The almost universal procedure for this is also one of the worst ways of doing it. You will probably be advised to float the bag of fish in the tank. Forget that advice.

Instead, take a fish-safe container of between half a gallon and a gallon (2 to 4 liters). Open the bag and gently dump its contents into the container. If there is not enough water in the bag so that the fish will be covered when it is poured into the container, begin instead by propping the open bag upright in the container, and do not pour out the fish until there is enough water added (by the next operation described), or try a smaller container.

Gradually add water from the tank to the container. This can be done by pouring in a half cupful every few minutes or by using a piece of airline tubing to siphon water from the tank. After the siphon is started, either tie a tight knot in the tubing or place a clamp on it so that the water merely drips into the container.

By the time you've added half a gallon or more, your fish will have adjusted to the chemistry of the tank water. At this point net it or them out and put them into the tank, then discard the water in the container. Do not pour it back into the tank.

Stress Management—Minding your Ps and Qs

The Ps and Qs of managing fish stress are Prevention and Quarantine.

PREVENTION

Preventing stress is what most of this book is about. Proper filtration, temperature control, feeding, and stocking of your aquarium, coupled with frequent large water changes, will eliminate most of the stresses that captive fish normally encounter. And, if you buy only healthy fish, the only thing left is to protect your fish against disease organisms—a practice otherwise known as quarantine.

The Instant Spoilage Factor

If you have a dog or cat and feed it dry food, you might set out a feeder with a week's worth of food in it so that the animal could eat any time it wanted. This system has its problems, although for some owners it can work out very well, but you wouldn't do this with a week's worth of canned food, since it would quickly spoil.

Well, the situation with your fish is even worse. Think of it in terms of canned cat food that spoils and produces poison gas—and which, when digested, is excreted into the litter box, where it also produces poison gas! That's the equivalent, since decomposing fish food produces ammonia, which burns the fish's gills and kills them, and even the food they eat produces waste ammonia when they metabolize it.

QUARANTINE

Quarantining new arrivals is a very important part of successful aquarium keeping. It can prevent disasters like a total wipeout of all your fish. It also, of course, requires at least two tanks, since you have to have a separate quarantine tank for the newly purchased fish. I have to admit that this topic caused me quite a bit of dissonance in preparing this book. As vitally important as quarantine is, it does not fit the mold of being a hassle-free step-by-step protocol for a first successful aquarium. So we need a compromise.

Aside from saving lives, of both your new fish and the ones already in your collection, quarantine can save you a lot of problems, and it can save you a lot of money if your collection is valuable. Since in this case we are dealing with your "test drive" in the hobby, and since we are insisting on purchasing fish from a reliable dealer who will not sell you fish that have not been acclimated in the store for a while, and since we are dealing with hardy, easy-to-care-for species, we can consider your first aquarium self-quarantining. That is, you are stocking just one tank, albeit gradually, so there is no existing collection to protect with quarantine.

It is important to remember, however, that if you go on with the hobby (as I hope you will), once you have several tanks and are regularly adding fish to a collection of increasingly valuable animals, a small quarantine tank is an ounce of protection against a ton of cure—and heartbreaking failure.

Recognizing Problems

Just what are the things that you need to recognize in order to prevent stressful problems from getting worse?

GASPING AT THE SURFACE

Know this:

- *No* fish normally gasps at the surface. Even air-breathing fish do not gasp at the surface.
- Fish gasp at the surface because they are suffocating and the water at the surface is the highest in oxygen.

- Therefore poor oxygenation (aeration) can lead to gasping at the surface.
- In a well-oxygenated aquarium, fish gasp at the surface because their breathing is hindered by parasites, damage to their gills, or toxins in the water.

So what's the treatment for low oxygen, gill damage, or toxins in the water? Water change! Quick, thorough water change (save a jarful of the original water for testing after you've relieved the stress on the fish with fresh water). Of course, if the gill damage (usually from ammonia poisoning) is irreparable, the fish will die, but many can recover when provided with ammonia-free water and high oxygen levels. That leaves gill parasites, which with proper selection and quarantine of fish should not be a problem for you but in any event can be treated for if they are.

That takes care of the *treatment*, but what is the *cure* for gasping at the surface? Eliminating the cause! Increase the aeration in the tank. Check ammonia levels and find out why they might be high.

Will You Feed My Fish While I'm Away?

It is a rare non-aquarist who can correctly feed your fish in your absence. Fish can easily go two weeks without being fed. Do not ask a non-aquarist friend to feed your fish for you while you are on vacation. If you will be gone for more than two weeks, either enlist the help of a hobbyist friend or, if you have to rely on a non-aquarist, pre-portion the amounts to be fed on a daily basis—and then hide your regular food supply.

CLAMPED FINS, SHIMMYING, HIDING, DASHING AROUND THE TANK

When fish do not act normally, it usually indicates a problem, often with poor water conditions or too low a temperature. Check these out immediately.

SPOTS AND SPLOTCHES, COTTONY GROWTHS

Red patches, fuzzy growths, and ulcerated pits are sure signs of infection. The fish should be treated with salt dips; if there is no rapid improvement, more aggressive treatment is needed.

Treating Problems

Medicating your fish is not something that you can do without help. You need to at least speak to an expert. Such a person—such as a good dealer—can then recommend the appropriate medication and course of treatment. Diagnosis probably would be more certain if the expert could see the affected fish, but taking the fish to an expert would no doubt add to the stress the fish is already under and could easily kill it.

Risk to the Biofilter

It is important to realize than *any* medication can harm the bacteria in your biofilter, and antibacterial medications obviously are extremely dangerous to them. Even if the instructions claim the medication is safe, it is important to monitor water conditions very carefully whenever you treat a tank with medications. At the first sign of an ammonia spike, you'll know the biofilter has been compromised and that you may be facing at least a mini-recycling.

Chapter Checkout

Maintaining an aquarium is easy.
- Get in the habit of checking your setup regularly.
- Many things deteriorate gradually and don't become readily apparent until a dangerous situation has developed.

Daily checks:
- temperature
- condition of the fish (and plants)
- appearance of the water
- operation of the filter
- overall status quo

Regular monitoring:
- water changes and vacuuming at least weekly
  - make sure to dechlorinate
  - make sure to degas
  - it is hardly more work to change a larger volume of water
- cleaning the filter
  - organic material in a mechanical filter continues to add pollutants until it is removed
  - a biofilter works best when it is not cleaned regularly
  - biofilter media should be rinsed in water taken from the tank to avoid killing bacterial colonies with chlorine or temperature shock

Feeding is the most important regular maintenance.
- It is important not to overfeed.
- It takes time to learn how much to feed.
  - So start by intentionally underfeeding.
  - Use this protocol to learn this important skill:
    - A fish's eye and mouth sizes suggest how much to feed.
    - Actually count out one flake per fish.
    - Observe the fish carefully as you feed them.
    - Be patient. You will get the hang of it.
- Vacation feeding is very risky.
  - In most cases fish can go up to two weeks without being fed.
  - If you must have someone feed your fish for you, leave pre-measured containers of food.

Health care is mostly a matter of prevention.
- Acclimate new fish properly.
  - Use a vessel outside the aquarium.
  - Slowly add tank water.

- Net the fish out and discard the water in the acclimation vessel.
- Stress management involves Ps and Qs:
  - Prevent problems with:
    - good filtration
    - proper temperature
    - good foods and proper feeding
    - proper stocking of the aquarium
    - frequent, large water changes
    - buying only healthy fish
  - Quarantine all new purchases.
    - Quarantine protects new fish as well as old.
    - A first tank presents quarantine difficulties.
- You must learn to recognize problems.
  - gasping at the surface
  - clamped fins and other abnormal behavior
  - lesions or growths on fish

No Bag Water

There is no benefit in adding the water your fish come home in to your tank, and there are several risks in doing so. If necessary after acclimation, add fresh water to top off the tank, but make sure to dump the diluted water from the bag down the drain.

Corydoras baribatus.

Part 4

Research and Planning

Okay. A lot of aquarium manuals would end right here. Of course, many new aquarists fail. Coincidence? Nope!

Now you're on an equal footing with a lot of experienced aquarists in terms of basic knowledge about aquarium setup and maintenance, but you still lack the finer skills needed to be successful. So here is where you will determine whether you go on to join the ranks of successful aquarists or go off unprepared, in which case you'll likely wind up failing at keeping fish.

The successful aquarist knows a lot about the fish he or she intends to buy; in many cases the purchase is the end of a long period of preparation and planning. In this part of the book, I will give you the information you need to make wise choices when you buy your fish, and I'll show you a large variety of ways you can plan your aquarium. This is the fun part, and you deserve it after assimilating all the information up until now!

Chapter 14

A Brief Overview of Aquarium Fish Species

I have to chuckle at the title I chose for this chapter. I could easily write a full book the size of this one with the same title! There are *thousands* of fish that are potential aquarium inhabitants, and hundreds of commonly kept ones. This will therefore be a fleeting overview, but not an inadequate one, since of those hundreds of aquarium species only a relative minority are going to fit all the criteria of ideal beginners' fish, one of which is to be inexpensive and universally available.

Some groups of fish, like killifish, are kept almost exclusively by specialist aquarists, but most groups enjoy dual popularity—with general aquarists and specialists alike. Once you have maintained a successful aquarium for a while, you may very well find yourself drawn to one or more types of fish as favorites, in which case you might just be on your way to becoming a specialist yourself.

THE FISH PYRAMID

You know that pyramid with the food groups on it? Well, we could construct one like it for aquarium fish. The relative sizes of the steps in the pyramid would reflect the general suitability of these fish for your first community tank. In addition they would reflect the relative numbers of fish in each group that are readily available at most dealers. Let's start at the base and work our way up.

Small, Active, and Colorful

The fish groups known loosely as tetras and cyprinids contain many species that form lively schools of colorful, peaceful, small fish. Although there are certainly exceptions, most tetras, barbs, and danios fit this description. Two notable exceptions are the big tetras known as piranhas, *Serrasalmus* spp., and the 14-inch (36-cm) tinfoil barb, *Barbonymus schwanenfeldii*. There are, however, dozens of common tetras, barbs, and danios that are in the 1- to 3-inch (2.5- to 7.5-cm) range and will provide a beautiful and dynamic display in your aquarium.

Tetras inhabit streams and rivers in Central and South America and in Africa, while danios and most barbs are Asians. They are for the most part from flowing bodies of water and have capitalized on the benefits of schooling. Because of this, many sport bright colors and patterns—even neon iridescences, which aid in school formation and maneuvering.

This schooling is very important to the fish. It is a pathetic and all-too-common thing to see an aquarium with an assortment that includes single individuals or pairs of species that are by nature schooling fish. This is bad for the fish and for their owners for a variety of reasons.

Schooling fish are under great stress when kept alone or in pairs. They feel insecure and do not display normal behaviors or coloration. Someone used to a singly kept tetra will often marvel when seeing the same species in a school of a dozen individuals. Its colors are brighter, and its behavior has changed from that of a flighty, skittish fish that swims jerkily around the tank to a member of a dynamic, chaotically choreographed troupe that roams the tank in constant motion. The fish not only move as one body but also are always on the move within the school, so the brilliant colors and reflective markings provide a spectacular display. In addition, any aggression will amount to little more than a bit of chasing or

Why Do My Fish Swim Back and Forth Against the Glass— Are They Trying to Get Out?

I once read an account of someone who used to forlornly watch the polar bears at the zoo as they walked back and forth, pacing incessantly in their little compound. Then he had the opportunity to observe the animals in their natural habitat and was astounded to see them doing the same thing on ice floes. It makes sense in a harsh environment for an animal to get its exercise in a spot already known to be safe and near a food supply, which may be why polar bears act this way. In any case, there are a number of reasons why fish exhibit "glass pacing."

Schooling fish often race back and forth along the glass. Remember that these fish are highly cued to get into a group with other fish that look like them. In this case, they see their reflections in the glass and try to join the school. They swim along vigorously, then come to the end of the tank, where they reverse—and so do the other fish! True, in the wild they might keep going in a straight line, but rest assured that if half the school reversed direction every couple of feet, so would they.

Another reason for glass pacing is for territory. Species that maintain a solitary territory will challenge any other fish within their boundaries. Often these territories are quite small. In this case, the fish sees a "rival" reflection in the glass and blusters up to it, chasing it back and forth as it matches each move of the other fish.

Rest assured that if a fish wants to get out of a container such as a net or a bucket (or away from a beak or a set of paws), its natural response is to jump, not swim back and forth.

nipping when there is a whole group, but with two fish, one will be dominant over the other, who may wind up severely battered. Therefore schooling fish should always be purchased in groups of at least six, preferably more.

Note that schooling species do not always school. For example, many tetras that school all day sleep singly, hidden away in the vegetation. When the lights come on, they come out of hiding and regroup. Many schools become straggly and disorganized as the group searches for food or plays games of tag, but let something startle the fish and they will instantly re-form the ranks. There is a lot of difference in this regard among species. For example, I almost never see straggler tiger barbs, *Puntius tetrazona*, but a glowlight tetra, *Hemigrammus erythrozonus,* school often lacks tight cohesion. All of this is natural behavior and nothing to be concerned about.

On Scientific Names

Got Latin?

Do you need to know your fish's scientific names? If your interest is simply in having a nice aquarium, you usually do not need to bother with scientific names. This is not because scientific names are not important, but because exact identification of the fish is not always important. If, however, you're thinking of buying certain species, identifying the species offered is very important, since several species can be called by the same common name. The best and surest way to properly identify a fish is by its scientific name. For example, "upside-down catfish" is a common name that is used to describe *Synodontis nigriventris* and *Mystus leucophasis*, two very different catfish with very different requirements (and temperaments).

A great many fish have no common name, and others have so many common names that it is impossible to list them all. Many fish come into the hobby without a common name and basically get a different name from every retailer who sells them. There also is no common name that is "correct" for a given species. For example, I recently ordered some "least killifish" from a wholesaler. In 50 years I have never seen that name applied to anything other than the livebearer *Heterandria formosa*. What I got, however, was a *Fundulus* killifish of some sort. And common names can mislead. For example, a huge variety of only distantly related species are all called gobies—a mixed group that cannot be uniquely identified through a single specific list of biological features.

Common names are useful in some circumstances, especially where exact identification is unimportant. The truth, however, is that once an aquarist starts to get bothered by not having a common name for every species, that person is almost always at the point in growth in the hobby where using scientific names is important. If the correct identification of a fish matters to you, you need to learn and use scientific names. If not, common names may suffice.

Are Scientific Names Difficult?

Beginning aquarists often complain that scientific names are hard to pronounce and to remember. This is a generalization that does not hold up upon examination. First of all, pronunciation is a non-issue, since there is no correct pronunciation of any scientific name, so you are free to pronounce it as seems best to you. There are many pronunciations widely used. For example, the loach genus *Botia* is often said both as bo-TEE-uh and as BO-tee-uh.

Botia almorhae, often called the yo-yo loach.

Are scientific names long and unwieldy? Some are, but there are plenty of counterexamples. One fish's common name is humuhumunukunuku-pua'ā, a Hawaiian name that is widely used and even has been immortalized in a song in a popular teen movie. Another long common name is White Cloud Mountain minnow, a name substantially longer than the fish! On the other hand, there are short scientific names like *Akko rossi* and *Lo uspi*. In addition, many scientific names are extremely easy to remember: the snail *Ba humbugi*, the nudibranch (naked gill) genus *Godiva*, the catfish *Zungaro zungaro*, or the wasp *Lalapa lusa*. Also, if you learn the meaning of a few Latin and Greek roots, many scientific names start to make a lot of sense.

Three of the four most commonly available livebearers are good fish for beginners—guppies, platies, and swordtails. Mollies are best left for when you have more experience. Platies are seen here.

Pregnant Fish?

Although the vast majority of fish in the world lay eggs (oviparity), some species retain the eggs within the body until they hatch and then give birth to live young. Depending on the species or group, there may be some nutritional support from the mother to the developing young (viviparity), but in many cases the fry develop solely from the nutrients stored in the egg (ovoviviparity). Some sharks produce an abundance of unfertilized eggs that the babies eat while still inside their mother, and a few species actually feature babies that feed on each other before being born!

You won't see any extreme behavior like this in your aquarium, but livebearing as a method of reproduction was widely adapted in a group of Central American cyprinodonts, one family of which comprises the popular livebearing fish in the aquarium hobby.

These livebearers are in many ways the backbone of the hobby, in large part because of their fascinating breeding behavior and the ease with which they are bred in captivity. The thrill of having your fish have babies in your tank has hooked aquarist after aquarist into a lifetime hobby of collecting and keeping all types of fish, but the original thrill never fades completely. With these fish, fertilization occurs internally. The male has a modified anal fin called a gonopodium with which he places sperm into the female's vent, and the female broods the young within her body. The babies are born fully able to swim and fend for themselves, and they are easy to feed. In contrast, the fry of many egglayers cannot swim for up to a week after

Livebearer Breeding Woes

The fascinating livebearers of the family Poeciliidae have a couple of adaptations that help ensure their survival in the wild but really louse up aquarists' plans for breeding them. First of all, the females store sperm and can have six or more broods from one fertilization. This means that if you don't like the first brood, you can't just switch males and try a different mating, since many of the fry will be from the original male. Second, the females can be impregnated when mere fry—a few days old! This means that babies kept in the same tank with their father or with other adult males basically grow up pregnant. Once again, this thwarts our efforts to select specific mates. The only way to get virgin females is to put the fry into their own tank at birth and then separate them immediately when the sexes become apparent. Since the fry do not all develop at the same rate, daily inspection and culling are required—yet another reason to leave breeding fish for a later time.

hatching, and they are very small and require microscopic live foods.

Unfortunately, livebearers often view their own fry as tasty snacks, as will all the other fish in the tank. Floating plants will give refuge to the babies, and some will survive if they have sufficient hiding spaces. Your tank is not a suitable place to raise substantial numbers of livebearer fry in any case. If after raising a few fry in your community tank you wish to pursue this aspect of the hobby, you can set up several livebearer breeding tanks.

Catfish

For a long time there were basically two types of catfish in the aquarium trade, a few species of the genus *Corydoras* and an occasional "pleco" of the genus *Hypostomus*. The latter were often sold to eat the algae that grow in a tank, but what they mostly did is outgrow the tank and harass the other inhabitants. Over the years, two things happened. First, planted tanks became much more popular, and no aquatic gardener would allow a giant plant-shredding pleco into his tank, even though the proliferation of unwanted algae was a constant threat. So the tiny algae-and-not-plant-eating oto cats of the genus *Otocinclus* became extremely popular. At the same time, new exploration and commercial exploitation of the Amazon basin brought literally hundreds of new species of catfish into the trade. Dozens of *Corydoras* and new plecos in a variety of genera flooded the market. Many of the plecos have a sort of hideous charm, but some are stunningly beautiful, and all of them have an appeal that draws a certain type of aquarist to the point that there are many people who specialize in catfish, having entire fish rooms devoted to these interesting creatures.

Although there are hundreds of species of catfish available today, only a few are suitable for your first aquarium. Almost every single one of the suitable ones is a cory cat—a fish in the genus *Corydoras*. These little catfish from South America are ideal aquarium specimens. They are attractive, active, comical, and perfectly peaceful, even more so when kept in the company of their own kind, since they are also schooling fish and are happiest in large groups. They occur in Amazonian streams in schools of hundreds or even thousands.

Although many loricariid catfish (the plecos) are sold for beginning aquarists, they are almost all a terrible choice. The one exception is the catfish of the genus *Ancistrus*, often labeled the bushynose or bristlenose cats. These algae and driftwood eaters (yes, they eat wood!) don't get enormous, tear up the tank, or harass their tankmates the way most other plecos do. In addition, they are diligent in keeping your tank clean of algal growths. It's hard to praise the appearance of these gargoylish animals, but many people describe them as cute in a sin-ugly way. In any case, you'll rarely see them, as they are nocturnal and come out during the day only if you drop in some tasty tidbit for them. Even if you have a lot of algal growth in your aquarium, it is important to supplement the bristlenoses' diet with vegetable foods. Parboiled slices of zucchini are a popular choice, as are sinking algae wafers. Place the food into the tank after the lights are out to give the *Ancistrus* a fair chance at it.

Sick Lids?

They're sometimes called "chick-lids," but the normal pronunciation of the name cichlids is "sick-lids." Whatever you call them, the fish of the family Cichlidae are among the most successful fish on earth. They have colonized an enormous variety of tropical and subtropical environments; there's even a native American cichlid. The discovery of and exportation of cichlids from the African rift lakes that began in the 1960s fueled the largest and most sustained specialist trend in the aquarium world, one that continues unabated into the present century.

What do aquarists say about these fish? Well, from a cichlid lover: *They're beautiful, intelligent, fascinating, captivating, wonderful...* From another aquarist: *They're big, nasty, destructive, mean, murderous...* Who's right? Both of them! As absolutely marvelous as cichlids are (I say, revealing my prejudices), they are almost universally inappropriate for beginners—almost. If you consider this diverse family of fishes, which has representatives in North, Central, and South America as well as in Africa and Asia, which has species adapted to soft, acidic rainforest streams as well as hard, basic mountain lakes and even marine environments, which has species that range in size from barely an inch to more than 3 feet (a couple of centimeters to a meter), which has species that practice many complex behaviors including adoption of young and brooding their eggs in their mouths, and which includes herbivorous, omnivorous, and predatory variants, it is not surprising that there are a few cichlids that are suitable for just about any environment, including even a beginning aquarist's tank. In the following couple of chapters we'll take a look at them as we discuss particular species of fish and outline some possible groupings for your tank.

FISH TO AVOID, AND WHY

I could fill a large section of any book with descriptions of fish new hobbyists should avoid and why, but in this book let's concentrate on which fish you *should* consider. I will list, however, several exceptions as completely unsuitable for your tank, simply because they are often recommended to beginners. As a beginner you should avoid these fish no matter what anyone tries to tell you otherwise.

Goldfish

Goldfish do not belong in your tropicals' tank. Three of the many reasons why this is so are: they suffer at tropical temperatures, they grow much too big, and they produce much too much waste. In fact, the space requirements of these fish is so great that in a 29-gallon (110 liters) tank without a heater and with double the normal filtration, you could house at most two goldfish properly. Goldfish are marvelous animals that have been enjoyed by aquarists since before there were aquariums. But leave them out of your tropical setup.

A fish to avoid:
Gyrinocheilus
aymonieri.

Chinese Algae Eaters

Gyrinocheilus aymonieri individuals are also sold without the Chinese designation as just plain "algae eaters," which is fitting enough considering that they don't come from China. But they're not the best algae eaters around, either. These fish are one of the worst choices you could make for fish for your tank, despite the fact that they are sold by the millions, mostly to unsuspecting newcomers. Experienced hobbyists know enough to avoid them.

These are real Jekyll-and-Hyde fish, starting out as algae-eating juveniles and turning into big, nasty, territorial eaters of the slime of their tankmates—that is, they do when they survive, but they often starve to death. Just say no to them.

Males Betta

Also known as the Siamese fighting fish, *Betta splendens* does not belong in your tank. Male bettas will likely languish and die a slow, painful death. The water is too deep, probably too cold and turbulent, and their lifestyle is adapted to an environment almost totally opposite that of a normal community aquarium. Don't do it to them, please. If the grace and beauty of bettas appeal to you after you've mastered your first aquarium, read up on these marvelous fish and set up an aquarium just for them.

Large Catfish and Friends

I have seen both baby redtail cats, *Phractocephalus hemioliopterus,* and hatchling *Arapaima gigas* offered for sale with absolutely no warning. Redtails are very large catfish, large enough to eat a cat or dog. They make fantastic pets, but they need a *pond*. I'm serious. To keep a single adult redtail cat you should have an indoor pond—an "aquarium" of *at least 1000 gallons (4000 liters)!* You must also have the resources to filter and heat such a tank, and the means of providing food for an animal that will eat as much as or more than a member of your family. Lacking such, please refrain from buying this fish.

The *Arapaima* is a primitive species that is another major contender for the title of largest freshwater fish on the planet, with specimens commonly 8 to 10 feet (2.5 to 3 m) long and reports of animals 15 feet (4.5 m) long! (Interestingly, the other major contender is the wels, a European monster catfish that looks like the stuff horror films are made of.) The cute babies in a dealer's tank give no evidence of their ultimate monstrosity. Most public aquariums cannot properly house this species.

Redtail cats and arapaimas are infrequently seen, but thousands of juvenile *Pangasianodon hypophthalmus,* "iridescent sharks" (actually a catfish), are sold every year, despite the fact that virtually none of them will survive to adulthood and full size of 2 to 3 feet (60 to 90 cm). Many new hobbyists will buy an iridescent shark, yet very few have them grow up in their tanks. If this fish nevertheless appeals to you, consider as an alternative the similar but much smaller debauwi cat, *Pareutropius debauwi*. This interesting 3-inch

The iridescent shark is widely available—unfortunately. It's a fish whose proper care is beyond many public aquariums with room-sized tanks. Avoid this species!

(7.5-cm) catfish is a midwater schooling fish, like *Pangasianodon*, and a group of six or more makes a nice display in a large aquarium.

Occasionally available are shovelnose catfish, sturgeons, and even electric eels. These and other gigantic fish do not belong in a beginner's aquarium. With adult sizes from 3 to 6 feet (1 to 2 m) or more, they would be unsuitable even if they didn't have special dietary and maintenance requirements.

Another catfish to avoid is *Sciades seemanni*, often called the silver shark, shark catfish, or Colombian shark. This is another fish that must be kept in schools, but it grows to more than a foot (30 cm) and requires brackish or full marine water, not fresh water.

FISH TO BE WARY OF

Of course you will be reading up on any fish before you buy it (right?), but here are a few tips to alert you right away about potential problems. A fish is unlikely to be suitable for your tank if it is in one of the following categories.

Mollies

Although they are often recommended, mollies do not make good fish for beginners. There are many other more suitable livebearers, and mollies should be reserved for a later time, after you have some experience under your belt. Mollies are not a problem fish, but they are sensitive to water conditions, and they require a lot of space. Many do best in brackish or salt water as well. Although there is some debate on the issue, I believe that the traditional advice to feed mollies a great deal of vegetable matter is still sound. Get some experience with platies and guppies before trying mollies, and keep in mind that if you want to raise molly fry, that is best done in very large aquariums or even a pond.

Sharks

There are a couple of freshwater sharks in the world, but there are no freshwater sharks available for your aquarium. However, several catfish and cyprinids with a general shark-like shape are called sharks. Most of them are a bad choice for your first tank. The worst is the iridescent shark spoken of above, but there are others, and most tend to be too large, too aggressive, or too demanding. The two most popular of the "shark" species are the red-tailed black shark, *Epalzeorhynchos bicolor,* and the rainbow, or red-finned, shark, *E. frenatum.* Both species are quarrelsome among themselves even while very young, and as they grow older they tend to start bullying other species as well. If you insist on getting a "shark" for your tank—and you might be tempted, because in good color both of these species are good-looking fish—get a red-tailed black or rainbow shark but keep only one individual, and provide it with a hiding place it can take over as its own little cave.

Eels

Likewise, you will probably not find true eels at your dealer, but you will find many fish with "eel" as part of their common name. Most of them are trouble of one sort or another, though in the case of the smaller ones (certain species in the family Mastacembelidae), the major problem is keeping these escape artists in the tank. Do your homework before buying, and pay special attention to adult sizes.

Big Mouths

A large swordtail, *Xiphophorus hellerii,* and a medium knight goby, *Stigmatogobius sadanundio,* are about the same size, but there is a vast difference in the size of their mouths. The swordtail is safe with any fish other than fry, but the goby will easily swallow most guppies and tetras—or even a small swordtail! It is safe to assume that any fish will eat another fish if that fish is the same size as its mouth or smaller, and I guarantee that you will be amazed by the extent to which many fish can stretch open their mouths. There are even species that can swallow fish as big as they are!

African Cichlids

Usually the term "African cichlid" is used to refer to cichlids from Africa's Lakes Malawi and Tanganyika. Those fish (and there are hundreds of species) are suitable only for beginners who are given instruction about how to provide the special conditions the fish demand. They should have very hard, basic, well buffered water, and their tank should be filled with rockwork piles that the fish can dart into and out of, which they'll do tirelessly. They are very aggressive, bullying, and highly territorial fish that will continually contend with each other for dominance, not infrequently to the death, which is one of the reasons why you have to provide all of that hide-and-seek rockwork for them. But they are very popular as specialty fish, and they have some big pluses going for them. For one thing, they are among the most colorful of the freshwater fish available. For another, many of them use a reproductive method (brooding of the eggs in a parent's mouth) that makes it easier for a breeder to feed the babies, putting them roughly on par with the babies of livebearing species in that regard. They also are undeniably very hardy fish if their water requirements are met, but they definitely are not candidates for the type of peaceful community tank that most beginners want and enjoy most.

There are other cichlids from Africa, however, and one in particular, the krib, *Pelvicachromis pulcher*, that might be a candidate for your aquarium. Beware of cichlids in general, however, and of East African cichlids in particular.

Man-Eating Catfish?

A fish collector, importer, and photographer brought an eerie story back from a recent trip to the Amazon. In an Indian village he was witness to an event that is an unfortunate reality of living along the Amazon River.

While some children were wading by the riverbank, a two-year-old was swallowed by a large catfish. Fortunately, the adults present were able to grab the fish, slit it open, and retrieve the scared but otherwise all right child.

The legendary piranha is not what these native people fear. They report being most afraid of stingrays, not because of the poison in the tail spine but because of the infections that typically follow an envenomation, followed next by the electric eel, which can shock and sometimes kill a wader unfortunate enough to contact one, and then large, human-swallowing catfish.

The Kiss of Death

The odd fish called kissing gouramis, *Helostoma temminkii*, draw a lot of attention. Although the wild green form is sometimes available, the domesticated pink strain is more commonly seen. Their everted thick lips are in a permanent pucker, and on occasion they will "kiss," with two individuals pressing their lips tightly together. This behavior is aggressive rather than sexual in nature, and it is not that commonly seen. It does, however, get a lot of people to buy two of these fish, usually to their dismay. Besides getting *very* large (a foot or so), the kissing gourami is a troublemaker, often harassing its tankmates, sometimes to death.

An Ugly and Odd Fish

A breeding account of the weather loach, *Misgurnus angillicaudatus*, reported success in "conditioning" the breeders by putting them in an unheated tank on the floor of the fishroom and letting the water in that tank evaporate almost to nothing over the winter, during which time the fish were not fed.

In the spring the tank was refilled, and the fish spawned happily. It's nice to know they're so tough, but that's about their only claim to fame, being otherwise simply large and nondescript.

Any Other Catfish

Any catfish other than a *Corydoras* or *Ancistrus* species, that is. Besides the oversized cats mentioned previously, many of the more moderately sized catfish commonly available are not good choices for your tank, either. Although cory and bristlenose cats will fit into almost any grouping, be extremely careful to read up on the requirements and traits of any other kind of catfish before buying one. Many are very large nocturnal predators and are often the cause of the mysterious Missing Fish Syndrome.

Cast Iron Fish

Some fish are almost impossible to kill. These toughies are, unfortunately, usually among the drabbest, least interesting species. One such example is the weather loach, *Misgurnus anguillicaudatus*. Juveniles are sold because they are said to predict the weather; what they do is become more active during barometric changes, and that is the sum of their appeal. You won't be surprised to learn that to condition most species to spawn you need to provide them with optimal conditions and the best of foods; well, not this one. Enticing them to spawn requires treatment that for any other species would constitute abuse!

There are also several species that can survive extended drought, either estivating in the mud like the lungfish *Protopterus annectens* or by crawling overland to another waterhole like

Doomed by Their Adaptations

Thousands of male bettas live short, horrible lives in little glass bowls, their life sentences determined by the unique adaptations to the Asian swamps they naturally inhabit. Being air breathers, they do not need large volumes of water to get enough oxygen, and being adapted to swamps, they can tolerate stagnant water. In addition, when a male sees another male (or his own reflection) he will flare his fins and gills and sparkle his dazzling colors at the rival. So people take these fish, put them into tiny bowls, and watch them display to their reflections in the glass sides. The problem is that the fish are kept at room temperature—much too cold for them, and the "water" they live in is mostly ammonia. I rarely see a male betta that does *not* have ammonia burns.

Misgurnus anguillicaudatus.

Clarias catfish. Sluggish bottom-dwelling predators are typically very hardy, and they often have some novel appeal, but aside from the fact that the "appeal" is often potentially fatal to you, the fish tend to be large, aggressive, and truly ugly.

On the other hand, there are some very hardy fish that do merit a place in the home aquarium. Not quite as tough as nails, these fish are very forgiving of less-than-ideal water parameters but still attractive. These fish include platies, most barbs, zebra danios, and white clouds. Many of the Central American cichlids (especially convicts) also are in this group, but they are not recommended for community tanks. Most of the popular species listed in the stocking schemes in a later chapter are hardy, though not cast-iron.

Chapter Checkout

There are thousands of fish species that are kept in captivity.
- Many of them, however, are not suited for a first tank.
- There are many groups that contain fish suitable for your aquarium, but research is important, as there are also many exceptions:
    - barbs and tetras
        - many small, colorful species
        - very active schoolers
    - livebearers

Marvelous Mollies

On the island of Kona, Hawai'i I saw the most spectacular sailfin mollies I have ever encountered. There were hundreds of them in several large schools in a saltwater moat used for passenger boats. The adults would swim about 1 to 3 feet (30 to 90 cm) deep, and a horde of fry would shadow them on the surface. In this huge volume of natural ocean water, these fish were of incredible size, finnage, and color.

You don't need a saltwater moat to have nice mollies, but you do have to pay special attention to diet and water conditions, and you have to give them plenty of room per fish; they are very sensitive to crowding.

- Guppies and platies are great.
- Swordtails are fine for larger tanks.
- Mollies are best avoided for your first tank.
- catfish
  - *Corydoras* are highly recommended.
  - Plecos are generally best avoided.
    - *Ancistrus*, however, are good for most setups.
    - The small oto cats are also fine.
  - Many catfish sold for aquaria are completely unsuitable.
- cichlids
  - This group is generally best avoided for a first tank.
  - There are a few exceptions, which we will cover later.
- Fish that you should stay away from include:
  - goldfish
  - algae eaters
  - male bettas
  - giant tankbusters
    - large catfish
    - *Arapaima gigas*
    - sturgeons
    - electric eels
- Fish that you should be especially wary about even though they may be recommended to you include:
  - mollies
  - fish called "sharks"
  - fish called "eels"

- fish with giant mouths
- African cichlids
- kissing gouramis
- catfish other than cory and bristlenose cats
- big, ugly bottom dwellers with special traits, like electric eels and stonefish
- Very hardy fish are good choices:
  - platies
  - most barbs
  - danios
  - white clouds

Epalzeorhynchos bicolor.

Poecilia velifera, the sailfin molly.

Chapter 15

What Type of Tank?

Just as there are different types of fish, there are different types of aquariums. The purpose for which a tank is being set up can affect the system as much as will the types of fish being included; in fact, the purpose often *determines* which fish will be included. Some of the following setups are unlikely to be first tanks, but all of them could be.

What Lies Ahead

• types of tanks for your
  first fish

Any division of aquarium types is going to be arbitrary to the extent that many people want to have tanks that serve several functions. The following list of tank types, therefore, is meant to present the various possible functions as independently as possible. You can, of course, mix and match from this list.

DECORATIVE TANKS

By far the most common, an aquarium designed to be an ornamental addition to your home's decor can take many forms. In fact, every single type of aquarium can be set up to function decoratively, though breeding and fry-raising tanks are less likely to be ornamental in nature. The typical decorative tank, however, has looking beautiful as an organizing principle.

Now one person's idea of beautiful may be another's idea of hideous, but that is true in tastes in paintings, wallpaper, and many other things as well. What is important in designing an ornamental aquarium is ensuring that the components selected to please your sense of aesthetics also combine to produce a healthy aquatic environment. Let's take as an example

A tank is whatever you make it. If it makes you happy and what you include in it does not harm your fish, it can be whatever you want it to be.

two tanks, each designed to house neon tetras, cory cats, a pair of kribs, and some platies. The first tank is meant to be as natural-looking as possible, while the second tank is supposed to match a purple and chrome color scheme.

Tank number one has a fine natural gravel substrate. A branching piece of driftwood forms the centerpiece, along with several large Amazon swordplants that partially obscure the wood. The rear of the tank is planted with *Vallisneria*, and pygmy chain swordplants populate most of the front area. Lighting is by several full-spectrum normal output fluorescents. The kribs have staked out a cavern under the wood, and the corys annoy them by playing hide and seek among the driftwood branches. The neons fill the tank in a loose school, but at the first hint of danger, they zip into the jungle of *Vallisneria*, where they regroup before venturing out again. The platies are a lively mixed batch of blacks and golds, accenting the greenery and contrasting with the red and neon blue of the tetras.

The second tank has fuschia gravel tiered with pieces of rose quartz. Plastic plants in pink, purple, and white form loose "hedges" along the upper tiers of gravel, and the center (lowest) section of the tank contains a silver treasure chest, a black and silver bubbling diver, and an air-powered volcano that spews purple sand "lava" in an endless recirculating stream. Lighting is with actinic fluorescent bulbs, which give an eerie bluish light. Along the back wall is a large turreted castle in gray faux stone. The pair of kribs can just fit into one of the turrets through an opening in the back, and they have spawned in there. The neons swim about confidently, ready to dive into one of the always-convenient plastic bushes if necessary. The catfish, when they aren't chasing each other around the tank, can usually be found huddled behind the treasure chest. The salt-and-pepper platies add a spot of dynamic silver color to the tank.

Both tanks meet the needs of the fish, and each meets the aesthetic requirements of its proud owner. Both are decorative and organized around the owner's desire to create a particular look.

THEME TANKS

A "theme" aquarium combines various elements around a central idea. We've just looked at a tank organized around a color theme—a decorative theme. The possibilities for other types of themes are endless. Some very effective tanks focus on geographical regions; they are called biotope tanks, and we'll look at them in a minute.

Besides colors, what sorts of themes can you use to design an aquarium setup? How about

Decorate to Please—Yourself

The only restriction on how you decorate an aquarium is what appeals to you. I myself have no desire to have human skulls, sunken treasure chests, toxic waste barrels, or medieval castles in my tanks, but ornaments in these designs are quite popular. On the other hand, most aquarists would find the bulk of my utilitarian breeding tanks boringly ugly, while I delight in sitting and watching the fish in them. So if you like the way it looks, and it isn't harmful to your fish—go for it!

Wood can be a beautiful, natural addition to your aquarium.

focusing on a particular group of fish? Or a tank in which all the fish are long and thin or striped or air-breathing or catfish or—a longshot, but possible—maybe even all named for a particular ichthyologist?

In Chapter 20 of this book some of the recommended stocking schemes are thematic. If you don't like any of them, come up with your own! The ultimate thematic community tank is, of course, the most popular—containing only fish that particularly appeal to the owner of the tank, for whatever reason.

BIOTOPE TANKS

Many aquarists enjoy trying to recreate a very particular natural environment in what is known as a biotope aquarium. The organizing principle can be as general as "plants and fish from Asia" or as focused as fish and plants from a particular location on a particular stream in Sri Lanka. Aquarists, especially catfish, cichlid, livebearer, and killifish specialists, are increasingly diligent in preserving strains, races, and subspecies, noting collection locations and dates, and keeping the breeding stock pure. For a first tank you will probably be satisfied with much less specificity, but later on in the book we'll list a few stocking schemes that are biotopic in design.

SPECIES TANKS

Some fish can be kept only in a single-species tank—they'll kill or be killed by any other fish you put with them. Many other fish, however, don't necessarily have to be kept separately but can be shown to new advantage when kept by themselves. This is especially true for schooling species, where the appearance and behavior of the school are as interesting as those of the individual fish. I've divided the stocking schemes chapter into community schemes and species tank schemes, so you will have several examples to consider.

INSTRUCTIONAL TANKS

It is very common for an elementary classroom to house an aquarium. While often it is home to just a few goldfish, sometimes it plays a significant role in the curriculum. I know of quite sophisticated setups in our schools, including marine tanks, breeding tanks, and native fish collections.

Aquariums can be tailored to the students as they progress. High school science classes are enriched when they include one or more aquariums with specific instructional intent. At the university level, aquariums of various types are used in conjunction with studies in ecology, environmental sciences, genetics, ethology, comparative anatomy, and various other fields, including, of course, ichthyology.

BREEDING TANKS

Although most tropical fish are bred on fish farms in Florida or Southeast Asia and some are wild-caught, breeding tanks are an important part of many aquarists' setups. Usually the term "breeding tank" is reserved for a tank established for the express purpose of propagating a particular species of fish, even though many fish will breed regularly in any tank. In a community setting, however, few if any of the fry will survive. A breeding tank is set up to maximize both the chance of spawning and the chance of survival for the young.

Is a breeding tank outside the scope of a simple first tank? In most cases, yes, but there are possible exceptions. More than any other group, it is the cichlids that come to mind when

Fish Tale

Tanks of native fish species, though they are not tropical fish collections, provide schoolrooms with fun and educational field trips, valuable lessons in ecology and conservation, and beautiful displays for the classroom. That's why in the United States, for example, The Native Fish Conservancy, a not-for-profit organization committed to the proper stewardship of native American fish species, is glad to assist educators with their Adopt-A-Tank Program. They can be contacted through their website, www.nativefish.org.

Cichlids will care for their young until they are grown and can fend for themselves. Here a firemouth cichlid, *Thorichthys meeki*, keeps a wacthful eye on its foraging fry.

speaking about breeding fish, and for good reason. Cichlids as a group are noted for their extended parental care of the young, and individual species demonstrate an enormous and fascinating variety of breeding behaviors. There are mouthbrooding species that keep the eggs and fry safely in their mouths until they can fend for themselves. There are species that start off with a few small batches of eggs until there are enough older siblings around to help protect larger broods. Some cichlids hang their newly-hatched babies individually on plant leaves like tiny Christmas tree ornaments. Some cichlids protect their newborns in pits they dig in the gravel bottom. Some cichlid parents chew up pieces of food and spit them into the cloud of fry they're protecting. And some cichlid fry feed on the body slime of their parents.

One of the stocking schemes suggested at the end of this book is a cichlid breeding tank, which will detail what it would entail to have a first tank dedicated to the propagation of a particular species.

FRY-REARING TANKS

Because of their utilitarian purpose, fry tanks are normally also utilitarian in design, very often containing only a filter, the fish, and water. High feeding rates and extremely frequent water changes are facilitated by a lack of substrate and decor, which could trap food particles.

Such does not have to be the case, however, and fry will grow very well in planted tanks—even planted community tanks, provided all of the fish placed together are of similar size. I once saw a beautifully aquascaped tank that housed schools of fry of several African cichlid species. It is unlikely that your first tank would be a fry-raising tank, but there are many interesting possibilities in which it would *start out* as a rearing tank. For example, some of the rainbowfish species are a bit more expensive than a typical tropical, but they can sometimes be gotten as very young juveniles at discount prices. When the only fry placed into a tank are the fish that will inhabit it as adults, the spaciousness (which may make the babies seem lost at first) will contribute to rapid growth. You'll need to be patient, but in no time your seemingly empty tank will be dazzling with color and action.

PET TANKS

Although it surprises many people, many fish become tame pets in the sense that they interact with their keepers. Both parties enjoy the interaction, and it is not unusual for such fish to mope when their owner is away and they are being cared for by someone else, or at least to show excitement when the familiar person returns.

Cichlids are the most popular pet fish of this type, but many large catfish are also kept this way. In addition, goldfish, koi, pacu, and other large species can be kept as single pets in a big aquarium. Many of these fish school naturally, but as lone pets they accept their human companion into their "school."

Whatever type of tank you choose, you must select fish that fit into the plan. In the next chapters we'll look at how to do that, and in a following chapter I present some ideas for stocking schemes to get you started planning your tank.

Chapter Checkout

There are many types of aquarium setups:
- decorative tanks that fit a particular aesthetic
- theme tanks organized around a single idea
- biotope tanks that imitate a particular natural habitat
- species tanks
- instructional tanks
- breeding tanks
- fry rearing tanks
- tanks for a pet fish

Chapter 16

Which Type of Fish?

This is going to be a very short chapter, since most of the topics have been or will be covered in other chapters. It's included for completeness and symmetry, since we are progressing here from an overview of fish to types of tanks to this chapter on types of fish and then to the next few chapters on selecting your actual fish, winding up with the penultimate chapter of the book, which discusses specific groupings for you to try. All of the advice here is general; like most other general advice, it will not apply in certain specific cases. It will, however, serve you well in most instances.

What Lies Ahead

- factors to consider when buying your fish

SIZE

Although you can mix fish of different sizes up to a point, in most cases you must choose between having all small fish or all large fish. Obviously you can have more small fish in a given aquarium than large fish, but often large fish have many appealing traits. Perhaps the most important point to make here is one I've made before (and will undoubtedly make again!): know how big the fish you are selecting is going to get. It is absolutely impossible to tell just by looking at it whether a 1-inch (2.5-cm) specimen is going to stay that size or become a 12-inch (30-cm) specimen. Here is an area in which your pet dealer's advice can be especially welcome.

TEMPERAMENT

Generally you should keep fish of similar temperament. That is, you can have a tank full of peaceful fish or one full of nasty bullies (in the latter case the tank will become "full" with many fewer fish in it). You can combine fish of slightly different temperaments to get an interesting tank, but you have to keep these concerns in mind.

BEHAVIOR

Behavior other than overall temperament is important, too. Easily spooked fish kept with active nocturnal species can become quite stressed. Likewise, having too many fish that like to zip around will disturb placid species that just like to "hang out." Fish that like to stake out a cave and spend most of their time in there are going to be hassled by active fish that like to poke around in caves. A specific case of this is housing dwarf cichlids with most loaches. The cichlids like to spend much of their time just resting in a cavern, but they will be constantly bothered by loaches, which are incessantly nosy and find any crevice irresistible.

Fin nipping is a common incompatibility, and it is often simply a result of keeping boisterous, fun-loving species with graceful types that have long, flowing fins. The slow-wispy moving targets are just too much for the little rascals to resist. The classic example of this is angelfish being pestered by tiger barbs. In this case, as in many others, the incompatibility can be greatly reduced by having a large enough school of tiger barbs, since they will be so busy chasing each other around that they'll pester the angels less, but it is never an ideal situation.

COLOR VARIETIES

Sometimes your choice of a fish species will entail a choice of color varieties. Although there are some naturally occurring color variants in a few species, usually the choice involves domestic strains. Although they may look very different to us, all the varieties of a given species are still the same species, and they will school and breed together. If you do not want this, you should choose species that have the colors you want, not different varieties of the same species.

PRICE

This one should be easy. Beginning aquarists should not buy expensive fish. Why? Well, some would say because they are more likely to kill them than more experienced aquarists, but there is another important reason.

What makes a fish expensive? It might be in poor supply but much in demand. What makes a fish scarce? It might be infrequently encountered in the wild, or it might be very hard to capture. It could be difficult or impossible to breed in captivity. It might be extremely delicate, with a very high mortality rate. Often scarcity results from a combination of these factors. In all these cases it is best to have some experience before tackling such a fish.

Look at the other side of this coin. What makes cheap fish cheap? They are usually easily bred or easily caught and not at all scarce in the wild (in some cases, though, fish found very infrequently in the wild will breed prolifically in captivity). And inexpensive fish are *hardy* fish! Every obstacle to keeping a fish alive tends to increase its cost to sellers, so the cheapest fish are also usually among the most likely to survive for you.

Of course, these are general rules. One exception is a new morph of a familiar favorite. For example, whenever a new angelfish variety has been produced, its retail price will be sky high for a short time, and the originators reap a hefty profit. Soon after the fish's introduction, however, many people will have purchased the fish and bred them, so the price comes down. Whenever an albino form of a fish appears, it enjoys a similar moment of scarcity—sometimes even rarity—and high price.

In some cases the price of fish is held artificially high through the actions of its supplier(s), who try one way or another to maintain a monopoly on breeding them.

Many small fish are available for sale, but some, like this shovelnose catfish, will start small but will keep growing and growing and growing…

Chapter Checkout

Fish can be organized into groups on the basis of several factors. These should all be taken into account when deciding on how to stock your aquarium.

* size
* temperament
* behavior
* color varieties
* price

Chapter 17

Stocking Rates

Here's the chapter I promised you back in our discussion about avoiding common pitfalls. Normally an aquarium primer has at most a paragraph or two on figuring how many fish to put into your tank, often based on the shortsighted "inch per gallon" rule of thumb. Here's an entire chapter on this topic. If you make sure you understand this chapter, you will avoid the most common pitfall of all.

What Lies Ahead

- problems and concerns with stocking your tank

THE NATURE OF CROWDING

All aquariums are crowded. Compared to natural conditions, fish are packed tightly even in the sparsest of setups. Good husbandry and maintenance practices allow us to keep fish healthy at many times the population density they would encounter in the wild, but there is a limit. Unfortunately, most hobbyists, and almost all new hobbyists, will overcrowd their tanks beyond this limit. Self-control on this point will be a major determining factor in whether you can succeed in the aquarium hobby.

I cannot stress enough how important this is. Remember that if you compare your aquarium with tanks belonging to your friends and neighbors, you might think your tank is almost empty. Please realize that the diseases, stunted growth, short life spans, and other problems that cause most new aquarists to quit the hobby are most often products of overcrowding. You would probably recoil from a 2-foot-square crate used to house four Labrador puppies, but the puppies would actually be better off than overcrowded aquarium fish, since their wastes don't pollute the air they breathe to the extent that fish's wastes poison the water they must live in.

There are many factors to consider when determining the proper number of fish to include in your tank, and they must be considered together.

Adult Size

All aquarium fish start out quite tiny, and almost all of them show phenomenal growth rates early in life. While there are a few species that grow slowly enough that it makes sense to think in terms of keeping the juveniles until they grow too large for your tank, many common aquarium species will reach adult size within a year or two from hatching, which in a few cases means going from a fraction of an inch to a foot or more in length.

Not All Fish Inches Are Created Equal

Overly broad rules of thumb such as an inch of fish per gallon are invalid. The major reason is that fish inches are not necessarily equal to each other—the bigger the fish, the "bigger" its inches are! That is because the mass of a fish (or any other living thing) is a cubic measure, whereas its length is a linear measure. Double the dimensions of a fish and its volume becomes roughly eight times as great, not just twice as great.

It is easy to see this principle demonstrated by examining various fish. A 6-inch (15-cm) fish is not merely six times as long as a 1-inch (2.5-cm) fish—it is also taller and wider, sometimes very much so. The heftiness of the larger fish translates into substantially more body mass per inch of length.

Since it is total mass that is important in figuring such things as oxygen consumption, waste production, and metabolic needs, you can see that a 6-inch (15-cm) oscar needs a much larger aquarium than six 1-inch tetras do—the oscar could swallow a half-dozen tetras and just show a slight stomach bulge.

It gets even more complicated when you consider different body types. A 3-foot (1-m) electric eel, *Electrophorus electricus,* is a hefty, meaty fish, but it is tube-like in shape, while a 3-foot pacu, *Colossoma* spp., is roughly as tall as it is long and is about six times as massive as the eel. So, you might figure, the pacu puts out six times as much waste, right? Well...

Waste Production

The biggest factor in figuring stocking rates is waste production, but this is not dependent on overall size alone. The pacu is largely vegetarian, consuming huge amounts of relatively low-nutrition food. The eel is totally carnivorous, consuming less food but food of a very high protein (and therefore nitrogen) content, and eaten in much larger single meals. Its waste, therefore, is more potent, more full of ammonia, than the pacu's. You can begin to see how complicated this gets, trying to figure out whether the lower waste production of the larger fish is more harmful than the higher waste production of the less massive fish.

Add to this the fact that two fish of the same mass/volume and feeding habits can differ greatly in the amount of waste produced. A sedentary ambush predator like some catfish will eat much less and produce much less waste than an active, schooling predator of the exact same size such as a piranha.

Electric eels are big and are not suitable for any home aquarium.

Behavioral Concerns

Still, it is not only body mass, waste production, and activity levels that affect stocking rates. Other behavioral factors must be considered. A 20-gallon (75-liter) tank might be overcrowded with a single 3-inch (7.5-cm) male *Melanochromis auratus* (an African cichlid) in the sense that any other fish in the tank would be quickly beaten to death. This is because this species survives in a very dangerous environment by fiercely defending a small area among the rocks, to which he attracts females looking to spawn

Even though pacus are sometimes mistaken for their close relatives, the piranhas, they are vegetarians, relishing various fruits, vegetables, and nuts.

but from which he forcibly ejects any other fish of any species, especially his own.

Take a much more peaceful 3-inch African cichlid like a krib, *Pelvicachromis pulcher*, however, and the same tank could easily house several other fish with it.

Similarly, a male of the very popular species *Xiphophorus hellerii*, the swordtail, can coexist peacefully with a large variety of other fish, including females of his own species, but a group of male swordtails will tend to fight a lot unless there are many more females than there are males. Likewise, a female swordtail trapped in a tank with several males will be terribly harassed by them.

The behavior of a given fish may change over time as well. One of the reasons I warned against purchasing a Chinese algae eater, *Gyrinocheilus aymonieri,* is that the docile juveniles become territorial bullies when older. Likewise, many small cichlids make fair community tank inhabitants until they spawn. But once they have a brood to protect, that quiet pair of cichlids may keep all the rest of the fish in the tank cowering in a back corner with ripped fins and missing scales, if not floating belly-up at the surface. At the same time, some dwarf cichlids can raise a brood in a community tank without decimating all the other inhabitants, so you can see that stocking must take a lot of details about the specific fish involved into account.

All in all, a great deal of information is needed both to determine a fish's suitability for your first tank and to create compatible groupings that will fit your tank both space-wise and behaviorally.

WHERE ARE THE NUMBERS?

All right, you complain, you understand the principles, but where are the figures for how many of each fish you can put into your tank? Well, there's a problem. As the material in this chapter indicates, there is no simple table from which you can pick one of these and three of those until you reach the total number for the gallons available. A choice you make can preclude other choices, and certain combinations are definitely preferable to others. If it were simply a matter of determining how large a mass of fish flesh a given tank can support without having the fish being asphyxiated or dying from the toxicity of their own wastes, we could come up with a formula taking into account body mass, activity level, and dietary needs. But that isn't what we're after, is it? The well-being of our fish, not how many we can cram into a particular tank, is the guiding principle; unfortunately, an awful lot of the calculations needed to determine what is best for the well-being of our fish are insightful and intuitive for experienced aquarists but not easily quantifiable.

Are you therefore totally on your own? Fortunately, no. In the next chapter we look at how to go about choosing fish in general, and in the penultimate chapter of the book I will present several suggestions for stocking my ideal 50-gallon tank, but they can be used for the more commonly available 55-gallon as well. That tank has approximately five more gallons of volume but half a square foot less surface area (the 50 is 3 feet by 1.5 feet, for 4.5 square feet; the 55 is 4 feet by 1 foot, for 4 square feet), so they're approximately the same in carrying capacity.

Chapter Checkout

There is no simple rule by which you can determine how many fish you can put into a given tank.

Several factors are important when defining crowding:
- adult size of the fish
    - Total body mass is more significant than just length.
    - Fish of the same length can differ greatly in mass.
- waste production
    - Size is not the only consideration.
    - Type of diet (herbivorous, carnivorous, etc.) affects the potency of the wastes produced.
    - Amount of food eaten is also important.
- behavior
    - Extremely aggressive fish fill up a tank quickly.
    - Behavior can change with age, nature of tankmates, and spawning readiness.

The next two chapters will provide guidelines for you to follow in order to create compatible groupings that will not overcrowd your aquarium.

Chapter 18

Putting It All Together

Now that you know quite a bit about aquarium setup and maintenance, about tropical fish species and about how to combine them (and how not to!), it is time to talk about actually purchasing your fish.

What Lies Ahead

- where to buy your fish
- how to buy your fish

CHOOSING A DEALER

In the online aquarium world, one of the common acronyms is LFS, which stands for Local Fish Store. The concept has grown so that it is often used to refer to a very special kind of aquarium retailer. Finding such a retailer is a major victory in your struggle to become a successful aquarist.

The hardiest fish in the world is a bad choice if it is already diseased, while more delicate fish in perfect health can be excellent aquarium specimens. Unless you are planning a collecting expedition to Brazil or Sri Lanka or somewhere else equally fish-productive, you must rely on your local retailer to supply your fish. You must also rely on his or her honesty to know what you are getting.

The original source of the fish, how they are transported, how well they are acclimated, and whether or not they get proper care once at the dealer all determine the suitability of the fish for your aquarium. If the fish have not been properly handled, they may not survive no matter how well you care for them. Much of the potential damage to the fish is not immediately apparent; hence your reliance on the integrity of your dealer.

The store with the lowest prices is not necessarily the best place to purchase your fish, nor is the one with the showiest displays or the most tanks or the greatest selection of fish. None of these things determines by itself which store you should choose. I have found excellent dealerships in large specialty stores, in aquarium discount stores, and in tiny Mom and Pop setups. What they all had in common was honest, knowledgeable, and dedicated staff—people committed to the hobby as well as to their businesses.

Many books for beginning aquarists go into detail about how to select healthy fish, how to inspect all the fish in a store to see whether they are sick or otherwise unsuitable. You don't need to do this, since you should have as your priority the finding of a reliable dealer. A reliable dealer will not intentionally sell you diseased fish, so you're way ahead from the start. Choosing a reliable dealer is a very important factor in determining whether you'll have success with your first aquarium.

CHOOSING TANKMATES

Besides getting healthy fish, you need to get compatible fish. It is possible to successfully combine fish from all over the world, yet sometimes fish from the same river can be terrible tankmates. This is where knowledge of a fish's requirements and temperament is important to have before you choose it for your tank. Again, your dealer can help with such decisions, and the schemes in the following chapter provide many examples to follow as well.

Species compatibility is, of course, of paramount importance, but there are other considerations as well. Most tanks look best when fish use all strata, so it is best to have some bottom dwellers, some midwater swimmers, and some fish that frequent the surface zone. Fish from different habitats like that are also much less likely to be incompatible, since they are not

A reputable dealer carries healthy stock. If your fish die after you bring them home, the dealer will usually help to determine the cause, whether it was due to illness or improper water chemistry in your tank.

direct competitors, and since they do not interact that much.

It is visually pleasing to have large and small fish together. As long as the large ones have tiny mouths and peaceful natures, this can be very effective. If we consider that most popular barbs, danios, and tetras are typically small, in the 1- to 2-inch (2.5- to 5-cm) range, then the gouramis of the anabantoid group are an excellent choice for the larger species. The *Trichogaster* species can reach about 5 inches (13 cm) long, but they are generally peaceful (if food hogs), and they are small-mouthed enough not to be a threat to most tetra-sized fishes.

There are other possibilities as well. *Pelvicachromis pulcher* is a cichlid suitable for most community setups. The males are significantly larger than the females and reach about 3 inches (7.5 cm) in length. Various loaches (*Botia, Chromobotia, Yasuhikotakia, Syncrossus* spp.) can be used, but you have to read up on them, because some reach sizes of a foot or more, and some can be quarrelsome and territorial even while still small. Others, like the yo-yo loach *Botia almorhae,* are about 4 inches (10 cm) long and fairly peaceful. These fish also tend to be less nocturnal than most other loaches, meaning you'll see more of them. There are some large characins, such as the silver dollars (*Metynnis, Myleus, Mylossoma* spp.) that are peaceful, though these herbivores are out of the question if you want a planted tank. Some large cyprinids are suitable for community situations, like the larger barbs or the bala "shark" *Balantiocheilos melanopterus,* but these fish must be kept in schools of at least six, and they get big, so very large tanks are needed for them.

Dyed and Dying

Dyed fish are quite commonly seen. Glassfish (various species in the genus *Chanda*) often are injected with fluorescent dyes, and they're not the only ones.

Aside from being extremely unnatural and impermanent, the dyeing process represents an enormous stress placed on a fish, a stress that can cost its life—which of course means that it might die shortly after being put into your aquarium.

There's no good reason to dye fish. There are species available in every color of the rainbow, and there isn't an artificially colored fish that can hold a candle to the natural beauties. The blotchy, unreal hues should signal to you that the fish has been mistreated. There are several varieties of genetically engineered zebra danios on the market that glow in different colors. These fish contain genes from corals and jellyfish that produce the fluorescent colors, and while you might object to genetic engineering, these fish can be naturally produced by breeding one fluorescent danio to another and do not represent a dyeing or injecting with artificial colorants.

Dyed glassfish.

CHOOSING INDIVIDUAL FISH

When it comes to choosing individual fish within a species, it is usually best to get fish that are about the same size. Depending on the setup and on the species, it may be best to get same-sex groups or mixed-sex groups, and the numbers of each can be very important. You might think it best to buy pairs—groups with equal numbers of each sex, but this is not usually the way to go. Fish that actually form mated pairs generally do not tolerate other pairs of the same species very well, and most other fish are either so docile that it doesn't really matter or they should be kept in groups where the females outnumber the males.

OFF TO A FLYING START!

Well, you've made it. You're ready to start getting that experience I've been talking about, and you're also equipped with the knowledge you need to avoid becoming one of those ex-aquarist statistics. The following chapter is chock full of stocking schemes. Find one you like, or modify one to fit your tastes. Then go on, and, if you remember nothing else, remember *patience* and *read before you buy*. Good luck and have fun!

Chapter Checkout

A good LFS (local fish store) is an important resource for a successful first aquarium.

- You should try hard to find a good LFS.
    - As a source for healthy fish
    - As a source for reliable information
- A good LFS:
    - Has honest, knowledgeable, and dedicated staff.
    - Will not knowingly sell you diseased fish.
    - Will not sell you inappropriate or incompatible fish.

Remember to be patient, to research before purchasing, and to have fun!

Chapter 19

Suggested Stocking Schemes

The best way to learn about various types of fish is to keep them, but a major source of failure for beginning aquarists is lack of knowledge about the fish they buy. Usually books to help beginners try to cram as much information as they can about many different fish into the text, along with a few rules of thumb for combining different species, but this book takes a different approach. Using knowledge built on decades of experience in the hobby, I'm presenting various groupings to try in your tank without explaining all the reasons for my choices. There is always time later for you to learn about other fish, but the goof-proof combinations I'm presenting are just what you need for a successful jumpstart into the hobby.

What Lies Ahead

- ways to stock your first aquarium

Of course, there will be many beautiful and fascinating species in your dealer's tanks, and you'll want them all. In most cases, however, you should resist the impulse. For example, say you really, really want a clown loach. Well, if you buy it, there is a very good chance it will quickly die. Is its beauty worth that to you? On the other hand, a year or two from now, when you actually know how to care for fish, a school of six or more clown loaches would be a marvelous display for you. Patience.

How about trying one of the following stocking schemes for six months? By that time a great many less-prepared newcomers will be those who have given up and sold their aquariums at garage sales. You, however, should be enjoying your aquarium more each day. After six months or a year of success under your belt, you can begin expanding in new directions in the world of tropical fish.

The groupings that follow are all setups I would pick out for you if I were able to go with you to your dealer to select your fish. They are not meant to be mix-and-match, but considered as a unit. You can make substitutions, but only after doing your homework. There are two variants for each scheme, one for a 50- or 55-gallon (200-liter) tank, and one for a smaller tank—a 29-gallon (110-liter). The numbers for each species mentioned are given in brackets like this: [6/8]. The first number (6) indicates the appropriate number of specimens for a 29-gallon tank, the second number (8) indicates how many to get for a 50-gallon setup. Note that in some setups more species are included in the larger scheme, so the numbers may remain the same for a given species (e.g., [6/6]).

Of course, for even larger tanks, additional fish may be included. In such a case, you might prefer to add whole species rather than simply increase numbers— more schools of different tetra species perhaps, rather than larger schools of the same number of species.

COMMUNITY STOCKING SCHEMES

In a Nutshell (SS1)

Platies, *Xiphophorus maculatus* or *X. variatus* [3/5]

Small danios [8/8] or giant danios [0/6]

Lemon tetras, *Hyphessobrycon pulchripinnis* [6/6]

Serpae tetras (various very similar species) [0/6]

Cory cats *Corydoras* spp. [4/6]

All of the fish suggested here are common and inexpensive. They can usually be found in most dealers' tanks, though you might have to wait for one or two new shipments for a particular species. In the event that your dealer does not carry a fish you have chosen, all of the species included in the following stocking schemes generally are common enough to be ordered without any problem.

Remember, none of the setups below will look like an average beginner's tank, which is a good thing! The average beginner's tank unfortunately is not successful. The successful groupings here are designed to avoid the pitfalls that uninformed impulse buying of fish can create, so you won't wind up with a let's-see-one-of-those-and-

two-of-these-and-oh!-one-of-them-too assemblage of fishes.

Stocking Scheme #1: A "Typical" Community Tank

This first tank is the most prevalent type. It pays no attention to biotope, meaning that there is no concern about mixing fish from different habitats—even different continents. It focuses on the beauty and form of the fish and how well they look together, and it makes a colorful if eclectic display.

Platies are used to cycle the tank in this scheme. They are available in a spectrum of colors and types—bright reds, metallic blues, blacks, pastel golds, long-finned, etc. These hardy livebearers will provide plenty of fry, some of which may survive.

Two or three schools of brightly colored active fish fill the midwater area of this setup. Danios (genus *Danio*) [8/8] will provide non-stop action, plus metallic iridescence. You can choose from the ubiquitous zebra danio, *D. rerio*, or the most sedately colored of the group, the pearl danio, *D. albolineatus*, one of the less commonly available species like *D. nigrofasciatus*, or one of the many new species that are coming into the hobby. For a 50-gallon (200-liter) or larger, you can substitute a school of giant danios, which is too large a species for the smaller stocking scheme.

Lemon tetras make up another school. The understated beauty of these peaceful silvery fish with fluorescent yellow highlights gives them their appeal. While by no means sluggish, these tetras will seem lazy compared to the energetic danios. Serpae tetras make the third school in the larger scheme.

The lower levels of this aquarium will be home to a school of cory cats. Besides providing a lot of comical action, they will also be on constant patrol, rooting out any morsels of food the other fish may have let fall to the bottom—but make sure they get their share, too. Although they will take food from the surface, sinking pellets or wafers are the best way to feed bottom dwellers like corys.

Stocking Scheme #2: What about Angelfish?

Few newcomers to the tropical fish hobby can pass a tank of angelfish, *Pterophyllum scalare,* and not want some. These beautiful and graceful fish are recognized even by many non-aquarists and almost seem to symbolize the tropical fish hobby in people's minds. They come in a variety of colors and patterns, in both standards and veiltails, which possess much-elongated fins. Unfortunately, angelfish are a poor choice for most first tanks, both because first tanks tend to be too small for angelfish (not a problem, however, for you!) and because angelfish do not mix well with many of the other fish typically chosen by new hobbyists. The mismatch goes both ways, with some common fish making life difficult for the angels by nipping at their long, flowing fins, and with the angels picking on or even consuming others. Here are two functional schemes that feature these stately animals.

In a Nutshell: Option 1 (SS2)

Swordtails, *Xiphophorus hellerii* [3/5]
Cory cats, *Corydoras* spp. [6/8]
Angelfish, *Pterophyllum scalare* [2/4]

OPTION 1

In this setup swordtails do triple duty. First, these fish (of which you should have either females only or one male and the rest females) will be used to cycle the aquarium. Second, they will provide beauty. I recommend red velvet swords or red velvet wagtail swords, which are the same intense red but with black fins, to complement the largely silver and black coloration of the other tank inhabitants. Third, the swordtails will provide frequent large broods of fry—irresistible treats for the angelfish.

A school of corys will provide plenty of action without harassing the much more sedate angelfish. The corys can be all the same species or a mixture of species.

Finally, small angelfish of any color and type complete this grouping. The angels will seem lost in here for a while, but only a short while. Given such uncrowded conditions, they

The beautiful flowing fins of angelfish will tempt notorious nippers like tiger barbs. Keep your angels with peaceful tankmates like swordtails, *Corydoras* catfish, and other angelfish.

will quickly grow to their full potential, at which time they will make an impressive display, gracefully lording it over the other fish in the tank.

OPTION 2

In this stocking scheme, a larger group of angelfish are reared together, providing both a beautiful display and the opportunity to perhaps produce one or more mated pairs. For this tank, the swordtails are eliminated, and the corys are reduced, because there's going to be a lot of angelfish mass in this tank by the time they are grown.

Cycling this tank is a bit problematic, since neither corys nor angels can be considered hardy enough. Remember our solutions to this problem, though. You can treat this as a species tank, which it almost is, and use some other fish to cycle the tank and be removed afterward. Or you could go for a slow cycling and make use of the size discrepancy between the baby angels you will be purchasing and the adults they will become in a year or so. With this option, you would start with one angel (body size of slightly less than an inch (2.5 cm). After a couple

In a Nutshell: Option 2 (SS2)

Angelfish, *Pterophyllum scalare* [4/7]
Cory cats, *Corydoras* spp. [3/5]

of weeks you would add one or two more, and so on until all have been added. If you choose this route, make sure to do daily water tests and to do massive water changes at the first sign of ammonia buildup. It will take longer to cycle the tank, but the fish will do much better. Angelfish are especially appreciative of water changes.

In a Nutshell (SS3)

White clouds, *Tanichthys albonubes* [6/10]
Gold barbs, *Puntius sachsii* [6/8]
Trigonostigma heteromorpha [8/15]
Dwarf gouramis, *Colisa lalia,* and/or honey dwarf gouramis, *Trichogaster chuna* [1 pair/2 pair]

Stocking Scheme #3: An Asian Accent

Southeast Asia provides a multitude of beautiful aquarium species. In this setup, we choose from different parts of this region to produce a lively, colorful tank of small fishes.

The tank is cycled with white clouds. This is a delightful species, extremely hardy, very colorful, and a peaceful, active fish. Two more schools of fish are gradually added, gold barbs and rasboras. Not only do the colors and iridescence of these fish complement each other, their behavior does as well, from the boldness of the barbs to the more retiring rasboras.

A pair of dwarf gouramis completes the smaller grouping. While many people want only the males of this species, the females have a subtle beauty of their own. Together, the red and blue of males of the original wild-type color pattern (additional colors are on the market today) combines nicely with the silvery greenish gray of the female. In the larger grouping you can use two pairs of dwarf gouramis or one pair of dwarfs and one pair of honey dwarfs.

Puntius sachsii.

Stocking Scheme #4: Fish That Are a Bit Larger

This aquarium is for those who want their fish a little bigger. Obviously fewer fish can be kept, but a very nice collection can be assembled to provide color and action.

This time the tank is cycled with blue gouramis. This species is available in many color morphs, including opaline, gold, blue, and platinum. You should have your dealer choose either pairs (male and female) or just females; this will make for a more peaceful tank. These fish are easily sexed by examining their dorsal fins—the male's is longer

Trigonostigma heteromorpha.

Tanichthys albonubes.

and more pointed. Being labyrinth fish, gouramis are able to breathe atmospheric air to supplement the oxygen they get from the water through their gills, so you will see them head for the surface regularly for a breath of air. They use their long, skinny ventral fins as feelers, and they can move them independently to touch objects in their environment—getting a feel for where they are, so to speak.

After cycling, the gouramis are joined by swordtails of any color type, and a school of rosy barbs. You can pick any swordtail variety that appeals to you, and there is no reason the two fish you choose have to be the same variety, but include at most one male. You will often see your swordtails nibbling on rocks, plants, even the sides of the tank. They are eating algae and various animals—tiny creatures that constitute a good part of their natural diet. Make sure that the foods you use have a high vegetable content, or else supplement them with an algae-based flake food on a regular basis.

The rosy barbs are truly beautiful fish. They suffer from the same prejudice as the dwarf gourami—people want only the males. In fact, the males often command a higher price, but that's fine. Simply buy fewer males

In a Nutshell (SS4)
Blue gouramis, *Trichogaster trichopterus* [1 pair/2 pairs]
Swordtails, *X. hellerii* [2/4]
Rosy barbs, *Puntius conchonius* [5/8]

Fun Fish Fact

It may surprise you, but angelfish are actually a type of cichlid. They share the same family (the family Cichlidae) with the kribs, convicts, Jack Dempseys, and oscars mentioned in this chapter.

Sex Discrimination?

The arrival of a new color morph of the rosy barb gave marketing experts a new toy. You will often find the new variety segregated by sex, with the males called "neon rosy barbs" and the females called "gold rosy barbs." The males command a higher price. The problem is that some males are slower to color up than others, so inevitably there are a few males in with the females. I recently bought four of these "female" barbs, selecting two that were starting to rosy up and two plain ones, and the morning after I got them, I had two pairs spawning in the Java moss in their new home!

than females. It will save you money, and you will have a more beautiful display. How, you ask? Well, first of all, a school of just females would be beautiful enough with their metallic silver sheen, but when there are plenty of females around, the males go out of their way to impress them, which means they will display their most gorgeous red coloration. With two males, they will always be trying to outdo each other, making for a very colorful performance. This species is also available in a gold morph, which is called "neon" for some reason, even though the iridescence is present in the wild-type strain as well.

This species can get quite large, and, in time, you might even have to remove some fish from the tank. If, however, you wind up with 6-inch (15-cm) rosy barbs, it means you have

Trichogaster trichopterus.

Puntius conchonius.

taken superlatively good care of them, and removing the other fish from the tank will leave you with a spectacular single-species display.

Stocking Scheme #5: From Deepest Africa

Here's a community that allows the new aquarist to enjoy the elaborate behaviors and personalities of cichlids without having the tank destroyed, and it combines several beautiful African species. The dwarf cichlid known as the krib (from the fish's now invalid scientific name of *Pelmatochromis kribensis*) makes an acceptable community resident.

It is important that you set up this aquarium with the kribs in mind. These cichlids do not usually destroy the aquascaping, but they do need a hiding cave, which, if things are to their liking, may become a spawning cave. An excellent hideaway for them is half a coconut shell with a notch for an entrance, or a similarly notched clay flowerpot having its rim side down. With more than one pair, it is best to provide *at least three* such caves, to minimize fighting over the best one.

The tank has to be cycled with fish that will not remain in the grouping or by the slower one-fish-at-a-time method. It also is one of the few stocking schemes that contain species you might have to hunt around for or special order—the one-lined African tetra. Other possible African tetras would be any of the genus *Neolebias*, all of which are small, peaceful, and beautiful. African tetras are not as common in the hobby as South American species, which could be substituted here, though the biotope theme requires authentic Africans.

> ### In a Nutshell (SS5)
>
> Kribs, *Pelvicachromis pulcher* [1 pair/2 pairs]
> One-lined African tetra, *Nannaethiops unitaeniatus* [6/12]
> *Synodontis nigriventris.* one of the species called upside-down catfish [5/6]

Pelvicachromis pulcher pair with fry.   *Nannaethiops unitaeniatus.*

This isn't a publishing error—it's *Synodontis nigriventris,* a catfish that swims and lives upside down.

A unique resident of this tank is the upside-down catfish. True to its name, this unusual clown spends much of its time belly-up. This is a special adaptation to feeding at the water's surface. Being nocturnal, this fish isn't around much during the day, but put some food in the tank and... zoom! The whole school zips out of its hiding spot, gulps down a bellyful, and zips right back into hiding. The larger females get about 3 inches (7.5 cm) long, but they often stay even smaller, and males are smaller. Although they seem to do okay singly, they are much more fun to watch in groups.

In a Nutshell (SS6)

Cherry barbs, *Puntius titteya* [6/10]
Black ruby barbs, *Puntius nigrofasciatus* [6/8]
Tiger barbs, *Puntius tetrazona* [6/10]

Stocking Scheme #6: Barbs, Barbs, Barbs

Some barbs can be a bit nippy, but this behavior is usually minimized when they are kept in schools. Some barbs also get quite big—6 to 12 inches (15 to 30 cm) or more. The species chosen for this setup all stay between 2 and 3 inches (5 and 7.5 cm). This tank should always be a lively and interesting display, with plenty of flashing colors and dynamic interactions among the fish.

Cycling is done with a school of cherry barbs. This perennial favorite is beautiful all the time, but during spawning (which will be quite often if conditions are to their liking), the males become an incredibly rich velvety red, which counterpoints nicely with the females' tan and black and cream.

When the tank is cycled, slowly build up two more schools of barbs, black ruby barbs and tiger barbs. The tiger is available in the original wild type, which is an orange-gold fish with black vertical bars and red fins, as well as an albino morph and a "moss green" variety, with new ones coming along. You can buy all the same color or mix them as you please—they're all the same species.

Stocking Scheme #7: A Tetrad of Tetras

Tetras are among the most popular aquarium species, and this grouping creates an impressive display with four beautiful and universally available species of New World tetras. All of these are small fish, not more than 2 inches (5 cm) long.

We'll use black neons for cycling. These little beauties with the oxymoronic common name nevertheless are exactly what it says—black and neon. They have both a glowing red eye and a fluorescent greenish stripe that turns an otherwise humdrum fish into a truly gorgeous animal. They are also hardy, active, and peaceful.

> ### In a Nutshell (SS7)
>
> Black neons, *Hyphessobrycon herbertaxelrodi* [6/10]
> Bloodfin tetras, *Aphyocharax anisitsi* [6/10]
> Glowlight tetras, *Hemigrammus erythrozonus* [6/10]
> Callistus tetras, *Hyphessobrycon eques* [6/10]

Once the tank is cycled, gradually add three more schools of tetras. The first is another perennial favorite, the bloodfin tetra. This is a streamlined silver fish with (of course) blood-red fins. A school of these fish is a very pretty sight.

The second school consists of glowlight tetras. This fish is true to its name, with a bold fluorescent stripe that glows a neon bronzy red.

Puntius titteya.

P. tetrazona.

Our tetrad is completed with callistus tetras, also called serpae tetras. These fish are stockier tetras, with beautiful red coloration.

Stocking Scheme #8: Another Tetrad of Tetras

Although most tetras are on the small side, there are several popular species that reach 3 to 4 inches (7.5 to 10 cm) in size. The species for the schools in this tank are chosen from this group, but we're cheating a little here in calling this another "tetrad" in the smaller version, since then you can keep only two schools of these larger fish.

Choose any two of these four species, six of each for the 29-gallon (110-liter) setup, and six of each of the four species for the 50-gallon (200-liter) setup.

Buenos Aires tetras are flashy fish with metallic iridescences and red highlights in the fins. Like all of the other fish in this group, they are active schoolers.

Bleeding heart tetras have a blood-red spot on the chest that gives them both their common name and the specific epithet of their Latin name. This and the long dorsal fin of the male give this high-bodied species a unique appearance. Diamond tetras, *Moenkhausia pittieri,* are true to their common name—these fish sparkle like gemstones. Although lacking a common name, *Hemiodopsis goeldii* is not lacking in appeal. Fish of this species can grow up to 6 inches (15 cm) long, but they are very thin, torpedo-shaped fish and are safe with all but

Hemigrammus erythrozonus.

Hyphessobrycon eques.

Hyphessobrycon anisitsi.

Moenkhausia pittieri.

the tiniest of tankmates. If you cannot find *H. goeldii*, you may be able to find one of the other species in this genus, any of which could be substituted. These are very active, very fast, very peaceful fish, and they are tight schoolers.

Stocking Scheme #9: A Black and White Tetrad of Tetras

This tetra tetrad creates a tank based on the visual theme of black and white (silver), but it is far from boring. The varied shapes and patterns of these small fish, along with colorful accents, prove subtly intriguing.

For cycling we build up the first school—of black tetras. This is a stocky rather than slender tetra, but still an active schooler. Besides two prominent vertical bars on the sides of the fish, there is a darkening from the second bar, just before the dorsal fin, through the caudal peduncle. This gives a half-black effect that is quite striking. They are also available in a white (non-albino) morph often called the white skirt tetra. Once these hardy little fish have assisted in establishing the biofilter, you can add three more schools.

The first of these is a school of penguin tetras. Two species are sold under this name, *Thayeria obliqua* and *T. boehlkei*, the latter of which is sometimes differentiated as the hockey stick tetra. Both are silvery fish with a distinctive black marking in the lower lobe of the caudal fin. In *T.*

> ### In a Nutshell (SS9)
>
> Black tetras, *Gymnocorymbus ternetzi* [6/10]
> Penguin tetras, *Thayeria obliqua* or *T. boehlkei* [6/10]
> Red-eye tetras, *Moenkhausia sanctaefilomenae* [6/10]
> Black neons, *Hyphessobrycon herbertaxelrodi* [6/10]

boehlkei this marking extends as a black stripe all the way to the operculum (gill cover); it is especially eye-catching, as it gives a first impression that the fish has only half its tail.

The next one is made up of red-eye tetras. As the common name suggests, this fish is accented by a red eye, but its overall color is a reticulated silver, with the scales outlined and distinct, and a broad black bar at the base of the tail.

Last is a school of black neons, *Hyphessobrycon herbertaxelrodi*, which do double duty by being included in this group as well as in our first tetrad.

Stocking Scheme #10: A Selection of Tetras

For this one you can make your own mix. Select four schools of fish [6/10] of small to medium-sized tetras. Some good choices are:

Adonis tetra, *Lepidarchus adonis*
Black tetra, *Gymnocorymbus ternetzi*
Black neon tetra, *Hyphessobrycon herbertaxelrodi*
Black phantom tetra, *Hyphessobrycon megalopterus*
Bloodfin, *Aphyocharax anisitsi*
Blue emperor tetra, *Inpaichthys kerri*
Callistus or Serpae tetra, *Hyphessobrycon eques*
Cardinal tetra, *Paracheirodon axelrodi*
Coffee bean tetra, *Hyphessobrycon takasei*
Colombian red blue tetra, *Hyphessobrycon columbianus*
Emperor tetra, *Nematobrycon palmeri*
False neon tetra, *Paracheirodon simulans*
False rummy-nose tetra, *Petitella georgiae*
Flame tetra, *Hyphessobrycon flammeus*
Garnet tetra, *Hemigrammus pulcher*
Glowlight tetra, *Hemigrammus erythrozonus*
Head and tail light tetra, *Hemigrammus ocellifer*
Jelly bean tetra, *Ladigesia roloffi*
Lemon tetra, *Hyphessobrycon pulchripinnis*
Lesser bleeding heart tetra, *Hyphessobrycon socolofi*
Loreto tetra, *Hyphessobrycon loretoensis*
Neon tetra, *Paracheirodon innesi*
Penguin tetra, *Thayeria* spp.
Purple tetra, *Hyphessobrycon metae*
Red phantom tetra, *Megalamphodus sweglesi*
Red eye tetra, *Moenkhausia sanctaefilomenae*
Rummy-nose tetra, *Hemigrammus bleheri*

Guppies are one of the most widely available fish. Any fish store will offer multiple color varieties.

Silver tip tetra, *Hasemania nana*
Ulrey's tetra, *Hemigrammus ulreyi*

These are all well known favorites, except for the Colombian tetra, which is a newcomer to the hobby and is found under a huge number of names, including flame tetra, blue flame tetra, red and blue tetra, etc. It is a gorgeous fish and a perfect community member, and a school of them can be an asset to almost any type of setup.

Stocking Scheme #11: Livebearers Only

A very impressive display can be made up of all livebearing species. Because the many different color varieties of livebearing species are of no importance to the fish themselves, a mixed group is of no real value for breeding, since the young will all be crossbred and probably not very colorful. When mixing platies or variatus platies *Xiphophorus maculatus* and *X. variatus*, respectively, with swordtails, *X. hellerii*, the different species will hybridize. Since, however, serious breeding is an expansion of the hobby beyond the scope of this book,

In a Nutshell (SS11)

Fancy guppies, *Poecilia reticulata* [2 pairs/4 pairs]
Swordtails, *Xiphophorus hellerii* [3/6]
Platies or variatus platies, *Xiphophorus maculatus* or *X. variatus* [6/10]
Bushynose cat, *Ancistrus* sp. [1/1]

Yasuhikotakia sidthimunki.

we won't worry about it here. Any fry that survive in this tank will be fine fish, but they are likely to be mongrels, or even hybrids.

We'll cycle this tank with fancy guppies, the traditional beginner's livebearer. Then you should slowly build up a population with swordtails (at most one male), any varieties, and platies.

Although not a livebearer, one *Ancistrus* catfish can add variety to the tank, and it will clean up any algae in it, including the hard-to-scrape kind that the livebearers just pick at ineffectually.

Stocking Scheme #12: Teeming with Tinies

This is another grouping that contains fish a little harder to find. All of them are well worth it, however, and with a little effort you should be able to find or special-order them. One of the appeals of a large tank of tiny fishes is, of course, that you can have more fish and more types of them. But there is another benefit as well from such a setup: the large schools you are able to have allow you to see more natural behaviors.

This setup starts with spotted danios for cycling. The rest of the fish are then added gradually and include the following species.

Fish in Trouble

Dwarf loaches are one of the many fishes considered endangered in the wild and surviving thanks to its proliferation in the aquarium hobby.

Boraras maculatus.

Heterandria formosa.

Celestichthys margaritatus.

- A school of Sid the Monkeys. This loach is the dwarf of the family, staying under 2 inches (5 cm) in length and usually offered at less than half that. It is an attractive and playful fish, one of the most active loaches you can find, and one that spends a great deal of time in midwater rather than at the bottom—a trait it has in common with the clown loach, *Chromobotia macracanthus*. Aside from amusing you with their antics and games of tag, these fish are excellent at rooting out the smallest morsel of food that their tankmates overlook, and they are constantly probing around to make sure they didn't miss any. Unlike other members of the genus, *Y. sidthimunki* will not outgrow its tankmates.

> ### In a Nutshell (SS12)
>
> Spotted danios, *Danio nigrofasciatus* [6/10]
> Dwarf loach, *Yasuhikotakia sidthimunki* [6/10]
> Dwarf pencilfish, *Nannostomus marginatus* [8/12]
> *Corydoras pygmaeus, C. habrosus,* or *C. hastatus* [6/10]
> Pristellas, *Pristella maxillaris* 6/10
> Pygmy gouramis, *Trichopsis pumila* [1 pair/2 pairs]

- A school of dwarf pencilfish. This attractive little fish sports horizontal stripes of brown and black with bright red accents on the sides and in the fins. It barely tops 1 inch (2.5 cm) in length and is an active, peaceful aquarium resident.
- A school of dwarf or pygmy cory cats—choose from or mix *Corydoras pygmaeus, C. habrosus,* and *C. hastatus*. These fish have all the appeal of the larger corys, just in a smaller package. They are also not as bottom-bound as their larger cousins, and they often school in the higher levels of the tank.
- A school of pristellas. These beautiful tetras are diminutive in size but big in interest value. Their schooling cue is a pair of white spots above and below a black band at the tips of their fins, top and bottom, and as they swim they scissor the fins into the body and then out, producing an interesting dynamic.
- Last of the tinies are pygmy gouramis. These delicately marked fish are about an inch and a half (3.75 cm) long and very shy, so they do not fare well with most other fish. In this tank of tinies, however, they will do fine. Unfortunately, they are not always easy to find. If you cannot get any, substitute honey dwarf gouramis, *Colisa chuna*, which get to be about 2 inches (5 cm) long.

Stocking Scheme #13: Tinies II

Here is another tank of very small fish. The scheme focuses on having large numbers of tiny fish. Some of them may be a little harder to find, but none are rare in the hobby. If you cannot get them through your dealer, aquarium clubs and online auctions are a couple of

Archocentrus spilurus.

possible alternative sources for many of them.

    Cycle this tank either by starting with the *Heterandria* or with a fishless method. The least killifish is not a killifish, but a miniature livebearer. It is a US native and a delightful fish for aquaria that don't contain any large fish to bully or even eat them. The females are just over an inch (about 3.5 cm), and the males are much smaller. The females are not large enough to carry a full brood of developing fry, so their young develop one or two at a time. Rather than dropping a litter once a month, they deliver one or two every day or so until they are all born.

    Perhaps the biggest recent frenzy in the hobby surrounded a fish which came in as *Microrasbora* sp. "galaxy," but which has been described as *Celestichthys margaritatus.* You may find these listed as either galaxy rasboras or celestial pearl danios. This tiny beauty is now being bred in captivity and is becoming widely available. Unlike most danios, this fish is territorial rather than strictly schooling. Typically a male and several females will hang out in a group near vegetation or other cover.

In a Nutshell (SS13)

Least killifish, *Heterandria formosa* [10/20]
Celestial pearl danio, *Celestichthys margaritatus* [10/20]
Boraras maculatus [10/20]
Corydoras pygmaeus, C. habrosus, or *C. hastatus* [8/12]

Mate Murderers

What sense does it make that cichlids often kill their mates? What species can survive if its members do that? The murderous ways of many cichlids are, in fact, a result of extremely well developed and adaptive behaviors. These behaviors, however, can have the opposite effect within the confines of an aquarium. The wrestling, sparring, and contests of strength that courting cichlids take part in naturally serve the purpose of making sure only the fittest fish reproduce. When a fish is too weak or is unready to spawn, it quickly loses in these confrontations and beats a hasty retreat. In your tank, however, this is not possible. In addition, the amazing fearlessness of the parents in attacking threats to their brood, which is necessary to ward off predation by other fish (often large enough to swallow the parents whole!), has no outlet in the aquarium, and the parents often turn on each other in a frenzy to keep away other fish—which aren't there.

If the fish are not crowded, male-to-male aggression should stay under control, but be ready to intervene if severe fighting erupts. These fish are *tiny*, less than an inch (about 2 cm) maximum.

Although I have listed *Boraras maculatus*, you can substitute any of the many other dwarf rasboras that have become popular in recent years. These are all an inch or less, and usually either red or transparent. They belong to the genera *Boraras*, *Microrasbora*, and *Rasbora*, though only a few species in the latter are in the one-inch range. The common names for these fish are creative and overlapping, being applied almost randomly to the various species. Fortunately their care is the same, so you can do well without knowing which actual fish you have.

The dwarf corys make the fourth school for this put-on-your-reading-glasses-to-see-them display.

Stocking Scheme #14: Starting with Cichlids?

Cichlids are one of the most popular groups of fishes, and they come in a dazzling variety of types, from tiny fish that live in empty snail shells to sharp-toothed predatory giants menacing enough to give divers a scare. They live in the Americas, Africa, and Asia and are found in all habitats and all types of water, from soft, acid rainforest streams to hard, alkaline lakes—some are even found in brackish or marine environments. Many are popular food fish in their native locales, and one—tilapia—is a commonly farmed fish around the world. They all show elaborate courtship and breeding behaviors, including exceptional parental care of the young. As if this were not enough, many are spectacularly colored, and most are very hardy nd easy to breed in captivity.

Unfortunately, very, very few of them are ver recommended as suitable for beginning quarists. The major reason for this is not hat they are hard to keep but that they are not suitable for beginning aquarists' tanks, which usually are community tanks. Few cichlids make good community fish. A great many of them are too large for beginners' tanks, and many are too large even for most other home aquaria, requiring tanks of 100 gallons (400 liters) or more for just one pair. Most are quite nasty, at least at breeding time, and many cichlids will destroy plants, break heaters, bite filter tubes, dig up gravel, menace any other fish in their tanks, and even kill their mates.

The fish themselves, however, tend to be cast-iron fish—hardy, adaptable, and rugged. This makes them good for beginning aquarists who are still honing

In a Nutshell (SS14)

Tiger barbs, *Puntius tetrazona* [6/6]
Cichlids for the 29-gallon [see text]:
- Convict cichlids, *Archocentrus nigrofasciatus*
- Blue-eye cichlid, *Archocentrus spilurus*
- Flyer cichlid, *Archocentrus centrarchus*
- Firemouth, *Thorichthys meeki*

Cichlids for the 50-gallon [see text]:
- Convict cichlids, *Archocentrus nigrofasciatus*
- Blue-eye cichlid, *Archocentrus spilurus*
- Flyer cichlid, *Archocentrus centrarchus*
- Firemouth, *Thorichthys meeki*
- Texas cichlid, *Herichthys cyanoguttatus*
- Jack Dempsey, *"Cichlasoma" octofasciatus*

Archocentrus nigrofasciatus.

Thorichthys meeki.

*"Cichlasoma"
octofasciatus.*

their husbandry skills. It is people's ignorance, not the fish's traits, that makes them such a bad choice for a first tank. You might succeed without knowing much about some tetras or platies, but if you don't know about the cichlids you are buying, you are almost doomed to failure.

On the other hand, many people have become life-long hobbyists because of initial successes with spawning a pair of common cichlids, which provides a real thrill. Thus in this guide there is room for cichlids, as long as you follow the protocol presented below absolutely to the letter. This setup is for a breeding pair of cichlids, but it will at least start off as a community tank.

The tank is cycled with tiger barbs. These fish will also serve as "target fish," providing the pair of cichlids with a focus for the aggressive tendencies that accompany spawning, aggression that otherwise can be directed at each other. Depending on the particular fish you have, the cichlids may get so nasty that you will have to remove the barbs for their own safety. It is also possible that the barbs will get bold enough to be able to eat the fry of the cichlids despite the cichlids' vigorous parental care, in which case also they should be removed.

CHOICE OF SPECIES: 29-GALLON TANK

There are four Central American cichlids that would work nicely in this setup. You can purchase a male and a female and put them together with some chance of success, but be prepared to intervene in the event that serious fighting breaks out. Some mayhem is normal in cichlid life and courtship, but if one of the fish is being severely attacked so that it hides at the top of the water behind the filter siphon or vertically in a corner, step in before you lose the fish.

With these and all other cichlids it is best to purchase a small group of juveniles and raise them together. That way they can choose their own mates, and harmony is more likely; the only problem is that you have to find homes for the others when a pair forms and spawns. A group of six to eight fish should yield at least one pair when they mature.

Which are the four recommended species? The first is ubiquitously available—the convict cichlid. This feisty little fish has maintained its popularity since the first days of the hobby, despite its aggressive nature. The reasons for this include its beauty and personality, as well as the fact that it is probably the easiest cichlid to get to breed—in fact, most people have the problem of stopping them from breeding!

Three color morphs are widely available, the original wild type, a dark-eyed xanthic (gold, white) form, and a marbled (OB) variety. This is one of the few fish in which the female is more colorful than the male. Both have a beautiful bluish-silver background with bold black bars (their specific name means "black striped"), but the female also gets a fluorescent green on the fins and a rosy-bronze fluorescent patch on her belly. In the pinkish variety, there are no bars, but the female's metallic patches remain.

In addition to these coloration differences, there is a size difference that becomes evident at an early age, the males being considerably larger. In fact, it is not uncommon to find pairs of convicts in which the male is 4 inches (10 cm) or more long and the female is barely 2 inches (5 cm). They do not have to be this large to spawn, however, since they will begin breeding barely past the fry stage. The smallest breeders I have personally ever had were a three-quarter-inch (20-mm) male and a half-inch (13-mm) female. They produced about a dozen fry and even managed to raise them successfully in a tank with other cichlids.

One additional sex differentiation is a common one among many cichlids—the dorsal and anal fins of the male are much more pointed than those of the female, sometimes gaining wispy filamentous points with age. Adult males also can get a nuchal hump—a fleshy protuberance on the forehead.

The second possible species for this tank is a very close relative of the convict, the blue-eye cichlid. Not quite as widely available, this fish is still easy to find. It is lighter than the convict and has a much less pronounced barring, looking almost like a faded convict cichlid, and, of course, it has a bright blue eye. The belly patch on the female is more copper colored, and when she is spawning her coloration changes dramatically, with the front of her body becoming solid black.

The third possible choice is the flyer cichlid. You may have to search a bit for this one, but it is not rare. This is also a barred fish, but both sexes go through a dramatic change, becoming almost completely black during spawning. Interestingly, the female goes dark when the eggs are laid, but the male does not darken until the fry hatch. The female lacks any metallic iridescent patches in this species, and although there is still a size difference between the sexes, it is not as pronounced as in the other two.

Last but not least is the firemouth. This species is a bit harder to persuade to spawn than the first three, but not much. True to its name, this fish has a bright red throat, which in the male extends to encompass much of the belly as well. During breeding the colors of both sexes intensify. Its care and management are the same as for the others.

Choice of Species: 50-Gallon Tank

Any of the foregoing cichlids would fare very well in a larger aquarium, especially since their broods can be very large, but with a larger tank you would also have the option of selecting your pair of cichlids from slightly larger species. The possibilities include the only cichlid native to the United States, the Texas cichlid, and the Jack Dempsey. Both these fish are more combative than the other four species, and it is unlikely that you can be successful choosing a pair of adults and placing them together. For these species you should consider the get-six-and-let-them-pair procedure the only choice. The Dempsey, named after the famous former world heavyweight boxing champion, is a pugnacious beauty. It is, however, no more aggressive than most other cichlids; it was named back when it was one of a handful of cichlids in the hobby, and the Texas cichlid is every bit as ornery—or worse. Be warned: if you choose these species, you have a good chance of winding up with only one fish.

Details of Tank Setup

This tank is designed with two purposes (successes) in mind: providing a nice display of a fascinating fish species and allowing you to witness the enchanting behavior of these fish as they raise their young. It is therefore set up differently from either a strictly functional breeding tank or a purely ornamental display.

Since part of the elaborate breeding behavior of these species often includes digging pits in the gravel in which they keep the fry at first, you should have a couple of inches of smooth medium-sized aquarium gravel in the tank.

You also need to provide shelters, first so that the fish feel secure, second so they have somewhere to spawn, and third so that the female can get away from the male if he becomes too rough. (Infrequently it is the male who is savaged by the female, and then he needs a hiding place.) These hideaway caves can be as simple as a sheet of slate propped vertically in a corner of the aquarium or as elaborate as a rockpile siliconed together to provide a latticework of small caves and pass-throughs. An extremely irresistible feature, especially for the convict and the blue-eye, is an arrangement in which two or more stones are placed propping up one end of a large slate, the other end of which slants down into the gravel. The fish usually prefer such narrow spaces (often placing their eggs on the ceiling of the cave), and they will dig and move the gravel around to fix things up exactly to their liking. Make sure that you arrange the stones so that their digging will not undermine the foundation and cause a disastrous cave-in. It is best to place the support stones directly on the bottom glass instead of on top of the gravel; that way the fish cannot topple things by digging under them asymmetrically.

You must always be ready to separate your pair if things get too rough. An effective tactic used by many breeders is to make a tank divider out of the plastic eggcrate that is sold as a diffuser for recessed lighting. A hole is cut into the grid just large enough for the female to go through, but not for the male. That way she can safely visit the male's side but escape to her own if necessary.

SPAWNING

In this type of setup, your fish should spawn eventually. Feed them well and keep up with those water changes and you will soon see courtship behavior. This consists of flaring the gills, locking jaws, and other tests of strength. The fish will then move on to spawning site preparation. They will vigorously scrape a surface clean with their mouths and probably dig several pits as well. Just prior to spawning both fish will extrude their breeding tubes; the female's is broad and blunt, while the male's is more narrow and pointed.

Although they usually lay the eggs in a cave, they may lay them on the aquarium bottom after fanning away the gravel, or on a rock, or even the vertical glass of the tank. The female makes passes over (or under, if the spawning site is the ceiling of a cave) the prepared location, deftly depositing lines of eggs. She is followed by the male, who passes over the eggs just laid, depositing sperm and fertilizing the eggs. They repeat this until all the eggs have been deposited and fertilized. Depending on species and on the size of your female, there may be anywhere from a dozen to a thousand eggs.

After spawning, the fish will care for the eggs, fanning them to circulate fresh water over them and mouthing them to clean them and to remove any fungused infertile eggs, which will turn white while the others darken as the embryos develop. They will also vigorously defend the eggs, even attacking your hand should you place it in the tank!

After a couple of days the eggs hatch, but that simply means the embryos break out of their shells. The fry are still a helpless, quivering mass. Each baby is still attached to the yolk sac, which provides all the nutrients it needs until it becomes free swimming. During this stage, which can last up to a week, the parents will probably move them from pit to pit, still guarding them ferociously.

RAISING THE FRY

Finally the fry rise up in a cloud around their parents, and at this point they must be fed. The all-around best food for them is live baby brine shrimp, but frozen baby brine shrimp is a

Pareutropius debauwi.

passable alternative. You will even be able to raise some fry if you feed them pulverized flake food. If you have chosen *A. centrarchus*, you may see the fascinating behavior of several cichlid species—the fry actually feed on the body slime of their parents.

It is important to watch the water conditions at this point. The fry must feed heavily to thrive, but that means there is a good chance of overwhelming your biofilter. Daily water tests are a good idea, and daily water changes are even better. When doing water changes on a tank with young fry, be careful to keep the siphon tube far away from the brood to avoid sucking them up.

The parents will continue to care for the babies for several weeks. If, however, they decide to spawn again, they may attack their young, so be prepared to remove them if necessary.

Stocking Scheme #15: A Triad of *Trichogaster*

The genus *Trichogaster* contains three popular favorites: the blue gourami, the pearl gourami, and the moonlight gourami. These 4- to 6-inch (10- to 15-cm) fish are all hardy, though the pearl tends to be a bit more fragile than the other two. Three pairs, one of each species, make up this setup—a "genus tank," if you will.

Xiphophorus montezumae.

Endler's livebearer.

We've already introduced the blue gourami. The moonlight is all-over silver, with reddish ventral fins; in the mature male they become blood red. These two species are somewhat aggressive, while the pearl is a little timid. Herein lies the only potential problem with this grouping, and you will have to watch to make sure the pearls are not getting harassed or kept from the food by the more boisterous blues and moonlights. A good way to set this tank up for success is to buy blue and moonlight gouramis that are considerably smaller than the pearls. They both will eventually outsize the pearls, but by then a permanent peace should have been established. The pearl's coloration is exquisite, with mother-of-pearl iridescences and violet casts.

Cycling is done with the blue pair, followed by the moonlights. When the ammonia and nitrite readings have returned to zero (or if they stay there for a few days in spite of adding the moonlight gouramis), you can add the pair of pearls. Technically, a 29-gallon (110-liter) tank is pretty much full with six large gouramis in it, but if you want some activity at the bottom of the tank (the gouramis stay pretty much in the top two-thirds of the water), a small school of corys is a possible addition—just keep up with those water changes.

In a Nutshell (SS15)

Blue gourami, *Trichogaster trichopterus* [1 pair/2 pair]
Pearl gourami, *T. leerii* [1 pair/2 pair]
Moonlight gourami, *T. microlepis* [1 pair/2 pair]

In a Nutshell (SS16)

Corydoras spp. [4/6]
Glass cats, *Kryptopterus bicirrhis* [0/4]
Debauwi cats, *Pareutropius debauwi* [6/8]
Bushy-nosed cats, *Ancistrus* spp. [1/2]
Upside-down catfish *Synodontis nigriventris* [3/5]

Stocking Scheme #16: Just Cats

This interesting tank combines siluriform species from all around the world, some bottom dwellers, some midwater schooling species, and even a surface catfish. A particular appeal of this scheme is that it emphasizes the diversity of catfish, which are often thought of as bottom-hugging scavenger-predators.

Cycling this tank is best done by one of the alternative methods, but you could start with the corys and use *very* gradual stocking. After cycling, the corys can be joined by one or two bushy-nosed *Ancistrus*.

The small and peaceful striped schooling debauwi cat is not a consistently stocked fish, but with a little perseverance you should be able to find this delightful species. These fish never seem to tire, and they provide action in the midsection of the tank.

I would not normally recommend the glass cat for a first tank, but in the larger version of this scheme, I've included a school of four. These fish need very good water conditions, and they must have plants or other cover to provide a sense of security. They are a midwater schooling species like *P. debauwi,* but the glass cats tend to hang motionless in one spot, always ready to streak away at the slightest provocation.

The top of this tank is populated by the upside-down cat we have already introduced in Scheme #5.

In a Nutshell (SS17)

Montezuma swordtails, *Xiphophorus montezumae* [3 (2 females, 1 male)/6 (4 females, 2 males)]
Endler's livebearers, *Poecilia reticulata* var. "Endler's" [4/6]
Danio kyathit [6/10]
Yo-yo loaches, *Botia almorhae* [4/8]
Tanichthys micagemmae [6/10]

Stocking Scheme #17: On the Wild Side

While there are many beautiful domesticated strains of various species, many people prefer the natural beauty of wild types. Often less garish and more subtle in coloration, wild strains deserve time in the spotlight as well. I should take a moment and differentiate between wild strains and wild-caught fish. Wild-type fish are the original type, and they look like wild-caught fish, but they may have been bred in captivity for many generations. A significant number of aquarists specialize in wild-caught fish, which are often expensive and hard to come by. This scheme concentrates on fish that are in most cases many generations from the wild, but they still maintain the appearance of their wild ancestors.

You can cycle this tank with the Endler's and/or the *Tanichthys*. Although Endler's livebearer has been described as a separate species, *Poecilia wingei*, most biologists consider it to be a population (variant) of the guppy. Because of its especially bright coloration, there are

Paracheirodon innesi.

P. axelrodi.

many strains that have been kept scrupulously from hybridizing with other guppies, making the fish very similar to the wild population.

The white cloud, *Tanichthys albonubes,* has been popular in the hobby for many decades, but its close relative, *T. micagemmae,* has been known to science only since 2001. Sometimes called the blue white cloud or Vietnamese minnow, this fish is extremely attractive. Juveniles have an iridescent stripe that positively glows; it is still brilliant on the adults, but the young fish are simply stunning. Both of these species are easily bred, and captive stocks are plentiful, but they are wild types that have not been selectively bred for any traits.

Montezuma swords are a wild relative of the very domesticated *Xiphophorus hellerii,* and they are increasingly available from private breeders. The males have extremely long swords, and their courtship ritual, which includes flaring the dorsal fin and swimming rapidly backwards, is fascinating to observe.

Danio kyathit is a beautiful 2-inch (5-cm) import from Burma that was first brought in around the turn of the century. It is now available from captive-bred stocks. It is worth looking for and should not be too hard to find.

This wild collection is finished with the yo-yo loaches, named for the markings on the juveniles, which often appear as the letters "yoyo" on their sides. The markings of the adults are also striking, though less orthographical. Yo-yo loaches max out at about 6 inches (15 cm) and are peaceful, but playful. The school will have a definite dominance hierarchy, and games of tag are a common pursuit. Not yet bred in the aquarium, these loaches are either wild-caught or produced in ponds in the Orient. The only drawback in this scheme is that these greedy eaters will probably make sure no livebearer fry survive. If this is a concern, substitute a school of cory cats [6/10]. The species doesn't matter, but it should not be an albino or long-finned variant, in keeping with the wild type scheme. This way, with a clump of Java moss or plenty of floating plants, some fry should make it. Besides livebearers, some of the *Tanichthys* fry have a chance at surviving to grow up.

SPECIES TANK STOCKING SCHEMES

A great many species of fish can be best appreciated when kept in a species tank with no other fish, and many others are seen in a new perspective in such a setup. Very often a single-species tank allows you to keep a much larger group of the fish, which often elicits behaviors rare or absent when smaller schools are kept. And, of course, this approach is best when dealing with species that are troublesome either with respect to their requirements or because of their overly aggressive or overly timid behavior. Below are a few schemes for capitalizing on the beauty and uniqueness of several popular species when kept to themselves in your aquarium.

Species Tank #1: Neon Madness

Neons and cardinals—those fluorescent bon-bons of the fish world. The bright colors of these two species—*Paracheirodon innesi* and *P. axelrodi*—seem to bring out the predatory nature of any fish that sees them. I have had fish not much larger than some neons I placed into a tank grab them and try unsuccessfully to swallow them. This makes it difficult to keep these species in a community situation, where they also do not compete well for food against more aggressive fish. The solution? A species tank!

I have an aesthetic reason for advising against mixing these two closely related fish: they are too similar. A large school of either (we're talking dozens of fish here!) is a breathtaking display, but if they are mixed together the viewer will be led to focus on their differences. Your tank will succeed either way, but it will look better if you stick to one or the other species.

Cycling this tank is a bit tricky and is best done without fish or with other fish that are removed after cycling is complete. Neither of these tetras does well with any ammonia. You can probably add the fish in small batches, say starting with only six and adding a few more at weekly intervals, but it would be risky. Keep testing the water and be ready to do massive water changes at the first sign of trouble.

If you have never seen a large school of neons in secure surroundings (terrified specimens in a bare dealer's tank don't count), you will be amazed by the beauty of this tank. While six or eight neons are certainly beautiful in a community tank, a couple of dozen of these tetras in a tank of their own are magnificent. In the 29-gallon (110-liter) version you can have 24 of either species, and in the 50-gallon (200-liter) you can have about 40.

Species Tank #2: Guppy Extravaganza

Here's a perfect setup if you like guppies, fancy or plain, one variety or many. These colorful little livebearers have been around almost since the beginning of the hobby, and they have been selectively bred into strains that bear only a small resemblance to the wild *Poecilia reticulata*.

Glossolepis incisus.

Melanotaenia praecox.

They have had a funny history, however, and the indestructible guppy of yesteryear is rare or even extinct today.

Nevertheless, if you purchase healthy stock from a reputable dealer or breeder you can have a very beautiful and interesting tank with these livebearers. (You will also undoubtedly have to find homes for their offspring, since guppies are not overly predacious on their young, and you will probably soon have a surplus.) This is a reason to buy all the same type of guppy, since crossbreeds among the different types are rarely as colorful as the original strains, and a group of guppies all the same color also makes a nice display. On the other hand, a tank of different color guppies can also be beautiful.

You should use about six fish to start cycling this tank, with a final tally of 24 in the smaller version and 35 to 40 in the larger. These can be pairs or more than half females, but it should not be a majority of males. On the other hand, it could also be *all* males. I have seen a very effective tank containing only male guppies of the multi-color delta variety, and it was beautiful. A tank of all males eliminates the problem of having too many babies. Although guppies are usually in demand, they are not expensive except for superior exhibition-quality stock, so raising them does not usually pay, and to raise good guppies you need a lot more than a single tank, whether a community tank or just guppies. Therefore, many hobbyists find the quickly reproducing fish getting more and more crowded in their tanks.

Do not, however, try just a few females with the idea of having only a few fry. A few females in a tank of males will be harassed, possibly to death, and the males will fight among themselves much more if any females are present. On the other hand, a tank of female guppies with only a few males will work very well. It will not be as colorful, and it will soon be overrun with young fish, but this is exactly the setup guppy breeders use.

Species Tank #3: Congo!

As an unabashed cichlidophile, I don't often have my attention consistently grabbed by tetras, but the Congo tetra, *Phenacogrammus interruptus,* is one that does. This magnificent African tetra is an opalescent beauty with a striking combination of blues, silver, yellow, and violet. With every turn of the body the light highlights a different color, and an active school of these fish is a gorgeous sight. A planted tank with a large school of *P. interruptus* makes a grand display. The smaller version calls for about ten Congos, the larger about 20.

Species Tank #4: Rainbows

In recent years, rainbowfish have become very popular. These Australasian species are beautiful and aptly named, though many are largely monochromatic, so you have to take them together to get the full rainbow. They tend to be larger fish as well as schooling fish, and they work well for a single-species setup, since even the single-colored species are radiantly beautiful, and you do not need the whole spectrum to enjoy their beauty. All of the rainbows are both colorful and active—perfect for a brilliant display.

You have a choice of species here. The first is the red rainbow, *Glossolepis incisus.* This fish is a bit too large for a 29-gallon (110-liter) tank, since it gets 5 to 6 inches (13 to 15 cm) long and is an active schooling fish. The 50-gallon (200-liter) can house a school of eight to ten of these beauties. This fish is sexually dimorphic, with the females being much narrower top-to-bottom and colored a greenish gray. The males mature with a decided vertical bulge, and they are a brilliant orange-red color all over. Both sexes have reflective scales, which shimmer silver on the male and gold on the female.

Platies are perfect fish for beginners. They are easily maintained, entertaining to watch, and readily accept flake foods.

The other possible choice of species is the dwarf neon rainbow, *Melanotaenia praecox,* which is only 2.5 to 3 inches (6 to 7.5 cm) long. Both sexes are a neon blue color. The males have red fins, while those of the females can be yellow to red. The brilliance of these fish is difficult to describe, and they make a gorgeous display. Since you can keep many of these fish in your tank, this setup is truly spectacular. The smaller version should house a dozen, the larger about 20.

Species Tank #5: Tigers in Your Tank

Since its introduction, the perky, colorful, hardy tiger barb, *Puntius tetrazona,* has been continuously one of the most popular aquarium fishes. It is a rare store that doesn't always have at least one tank full of them. And they are best appreciated in a large school, such as you could keep in a species tank. They are not aggressive, but they are pesky fin-nippers at times, which is another reason to keep them to themselves. You can house 12 to 15 tigers in the 29-gallon, up to two dozen in the 50.

Species Tank #6: Platies Galore

Platies do not school as cohesively as tetras or danios, but they get along very well and swim together in loose groups—even if sometimes it is just two or three males chasing a female. Because they come in a variety of types, it is possible to sample the market and produce a tank of pairs, each of them a different variety; in fact, each of the fish could be a different variety! The smaller tank can handle up to eight pairs of platies, the larger up to 15 pairs.

This is not to say that you shouldn't get all the platies the same color. This is especially effective with varieties that have bold markings, such as wagtails with their intense colors and black fins or tuxedos, which are black surrounded by color. Although I still see plenty of red wagtail platies, it's been a long time since I've seen the gold wagtail platy of 30 years ago. If you could find them, a mixture of gold wagtails and red wagtails would also be a fantastic display.

Of course, if you want to save any of the babies born in your tank, and you want them to be true to type, you must get all the same variety of platy, and you must not buy them from a mixed tank, since the females will already have been bred by males of a different color.

Species Tank #7: Delightful Danios

This scheme makes use of the plethora of "new" danios, those that have been brought into the hobby in recent years as various new Southeast Asian markets, like Burma and Vietnam, have opened up. The identification and taxonomy of many of these species is far from sorted out, so they are often given temporary names. Just one example are the fish initially called *Danio* sp. "Hikari yellow" and *Danio* sp. "Hikari blue." Although at first thought to be two separate species, it turns out that they are the male and female of the same species.

These new imports are often given creative names by distributors, so it may be difficult to determine exactly what is being offered. Fortunately their required care is similar, so if you find one you like, substitute it in this stocking scheme. Of course, this setup will work as well with the common danios that have been around for years; in fact, it is very hard to beat a species tank of zebra danios for a vibrant and dynamic display.

There have been a couple of new giant danio species introduced (typically in the genus *Devario*), but most have been small, the size of zebra danios or even smaller, and we concentrate on those here. This species tank can be planted, but it should have plenty of open swimming room. Since this is a single-species setup, the fish will become bolder as they realize they are alone.

It is easy to cycle this tank by starting with a few danios and adding a few more each week, but remember to test the water daily to avoid nasty surprises.

Species Tank #8: A Wet Pet

Earlier in this book I mentioned the appeal of baby oscars, *Astronotus ocellatus,* and the catastrophe their purchase is for unsuspecting newcomers. The little guys are really cute. Many aquarists find the adults cute, too, even at their tank-busting size of a foot (30 cm) or more.

Just How Big Is a Fish Brain Anyway?

Although many species of fish show considerable intelligence, none is going to score very high on an IQ test. This is because fish are mostly instinct driven. This can sometimes make them appear smart. For example, some sedentary species will lie on the bottom, wiggling a fin or a fleshy appendage like a worm. When another fish comes to snatch the wriggly snack, it instead becomes the first fish's dinner.

Other times, the same instinctive drives make them appear too dumb for words. For example, some fish, like kuhli loaches, are notorious for getting stuck (and sometimes killed) in siphon tubes, under undergravel filter plates, inside tank ornaments, etc.

The thing is, in both cases what impresses us is merely instinct. The "clever" angler doesn't think about what it's doing, and the poor "suicidal" loach is merely following instinctive drives to seek out tiny crevices where it can hide safely from predators. In the latter case, however, the artificial environment of the aquarium often offers death rather than safety in tiny crevices.

In general, large predatory species like cichlids and catfish, for whom learning the habits of prey species is a matter of life and death, show much more insightful behavior, and they often have a "personality" that endears them to their keepers.

Not only are they very attractive, they are extremely personable pets.

Yes, you read that correctly. Oscars, like many other large cichlids, show an incredible intelligence and actually will interact with you. A pet oscar learns to recognize the person who feeds it, and some even enjoy being petted or gently stroked. It will eat from your hand, literally jumping out of the water to grab a choice morsel. Speaking of which, make sure that your tank is securely covered. The hinged opening on a regular aquarium hood will need to be weighted down to prevent the large cichlid from jumping through it to its doom.

Oscars are not difficult fish to keep, provided you follow a few simple rules:

- A 29-gallon (110-liter) tank is large enough for *one oscar only*. Just one. No matter what! A 50-gallon or 55-gallon (200-liter) can handle two, but it works very well for just one, also.
- You should have no gravel in the tank. A bare-bottomed tank is much easier to keep clean, and oscars are *messy*. When they eat, they chew their food, and particles come spewing out of the gills. They will often chew, spit the food out, and suck it into the mouth again for more chewing. You will have to siphon the bottom clean frequently, probably after each feeding.

Oscars are usually quite friendly and tame, though when very young your pet might be timid unless given a few rocks or plastic plants to hide behind. Once it is familiar with you, it will not require any tank decor. If you want some large rocks for aesthetic reasons, that is fine, but make sure they are big enough—oscars are capable of pushing some very large stones around the tank, scratching the bottom glass and perhaps even cracking the tank.

If you have the means to keep them and are drawn to larger fish, oscars are a perfect choice.

- You must have increased filtration on the tank, preferably with two filters. One very powerful filter could handle the 29, but two such filters would be superb on the 50. You see, we're actually stretching things a bit here with these very large fish, and extra filtration and water changes help extend the capacity of your tank.
- You must change at least half of the water twice

Oscars start out small but can exceed 12 inches (30 cm).

a week, preferably more, preferably more often. If you don't, your oscar is sure to get hole-in-head disease, or worse. Just do the water changes—your oscar will love you for it. Mine dance with glee when they see the hose coming, and they play in the stream of fresh water, obviously experiencing pleasure. Daily water changes are perfect for these fish, if you can manage them.

- You should not overfeed your oscar. While it is growing it should be fed like any other fish, small amounts several times a day, but once it is mature, three times a week is sufficient. It will gladly eat a great deal more, but it will suffer for it in the long run, and the tank will be much harder to keep clean.

- Never—repeat *never*—buy feeder fish to give to your oscar. It will certainly enjoy hunting them down and sucking them in, but remember that the chance of eventually transmitting parasites or disease to your pet is so great that it is almost inevitable, and feeder fish are not a good choice nutritionally either. I have seen too many once-beautiful fish destroyed by a feeder fish diet.

So what *do* you feed a pet oscar? There are many commercial foods especially formulated for large cichlids—pellets and sticks of the same types of food that are made into flakes for smaller fish. A particular favorite of oscars is freeze-dried krill, which are too large for many fish, but not for oscars! Earthworms are relished, as are crickets. Raw ground turkey is also a good choice for varying the diet, but avoid ground beef, which is much fattier.

- Your oscar will need toys. Toys? Yes, these intelligent fish can easily get bored, and if bored, they do things like disconnect filter tubes and break aquarium heaters. Much of this behavior is frustrated digging impulses, and in a gravel-bottomed tank they spend a lot of time digging pits and moving the gravel piles around. I've already indicated, however, that gravel in an oscar tank presents a major hygiene problem. You can give your oscar a handful of gravel to play with. Sometimes they can become engrossed in constantly rearranging this bit of gravel, but it is not enough to interfere with keeping the tank clean.

Another possible toy for your oscar is a large plastic plant. The plant will bob around the tank, and the oscar can bite it, chase it, and shake it to its heart's content. It would, of course, do the same thing to a live plant, shredding it completely in most cases. Many oscars like to play with a ping pong ball in the same way.

A mirror placed against the side of the tank may give your fish some "interaction" with its reflection. If, however, your oscar becomes overly aggressive toward the image, charging it incessantly, you should remove the mirror. Some gill flaring and mouthing of the glass is fine, but if the fish is obviously becoming irritated, you should intervene to prevent it from hurting itself.

Attention from you is also necessary to keep your fish happy. Oscars are fairly social fish, but you need an immense aquarium to keep several, so a lone fish will enjoy interacting with humans. This does not have to be physical interaction, though many large cichlids do enjoy a gentle rubdown from their owners. You can become good friends through the glass. Even just sitting near the aquarium and reading or doing paperwork will provide your fish with something interesting to watch, and it will be always aware of what's going on in the room.

You might be wondering what happens if you decide to keep two oscars. Chances are that if they are raised together, they will get along. If they are male and female, they might even spawn. Actually, they might spawn (that is, lay eggs) if you have two females. The biggest chance of a problem is if you wind up with two males, but in the absence of a female to fight over, they will probably be buddies. By the way, you won't be able to tell the sex of your oscars—but they will!

Chapter Checkout

You can avoid a great many unforeseen problems if you use one of the stocking schemes in this chapter for your first aquarium. They have all been vetted for compatibility and other issues.

What About My Goldfish? What About My Betta?

Notice how neither goldfish nor bettas (Siamese fighting fish) were mentioned as a stocking recommendation in this chapter. Remember, both types have specific temperature requirements outside of those of most tropical fish—goldfish prefer colder water, bettas warmer. Detailing setups for these popular and ubiquitous fish is outside the scope of this book, but others are available that do just this.

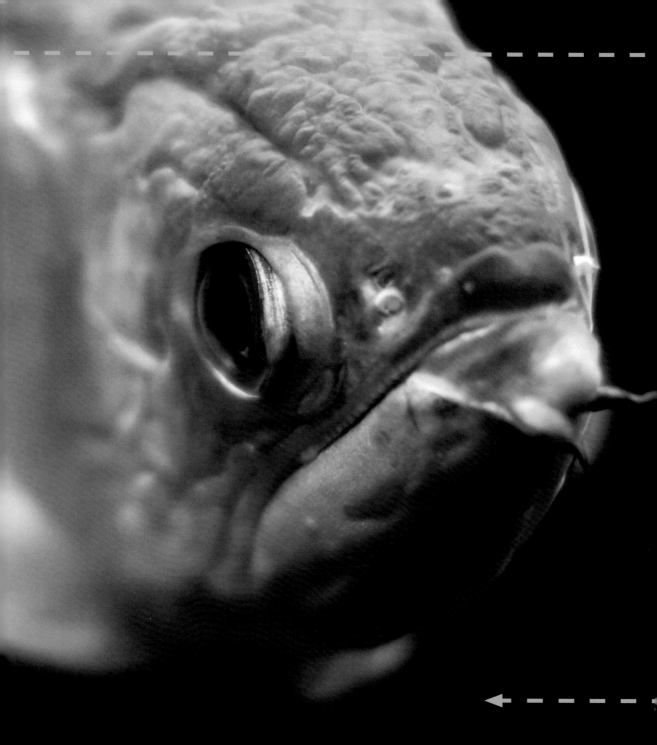

Chapter 20

Choices

Now it's up to you. You have in your hands a guide to the amazing world of freshwater aquariums. I have done my best to bring you a simple yet complete protocol that just about guarantees success with your first fish tank. If you choose to follow it, you will enjoy your first aquarium, and you'll likely have an enjoyable and educational hobby for the rest of your life.

Aquarium societies will often hold auctions where you can bid on fish, food, supplies, and more. Such organizations are an excellent resource for you. Pictured here is an auction held by the Jeresy Shore Aquarium Society.

We've discussed that statistically the cards are stacked against you as a new aquarist. But while most beginners quit the hobby in the first year, this book lets you buck those odds. However, it still leaves you with only rudimentary knowledge about various aquarium topics. This means that once you have that first successful aquarium up and running you will have plenty of options for how to proceed. More than anything, I hope I have convinced you of the importance of researching before purchasing—whether equipment or livestock—and of the importance of…you know it, lots of large water changes!

In closing I want to mention a couple of resources that you can use as continued support as you succeed with your first aquarium and continue in the hobby.

AQUARIUM SOCIETIES

An excellent idea at this point is to join a club. Local aquarium clubs can provide you with plenty of useful information, as well as serving as a source for equipment, plants, and fish. On top of this, they offer the fellowship and camaraderie that are experienced whenever people who share a passion for fish gather. If there is no local club, consider starting one! I guarantee there are aquarium hobbyists in your area, even if they are not yet organized.

Something for Everyone

There are so many freshwater fish available in the hobby that there is literally something for everyone. Once you master basic husbandry techniques you can seek out one or more of these fascinating species. Be sure to research the fish extensively before purchase and remember, have fun!

RESEARCH

This is truly the Information Age, and there is a seemingly endless variety of books and websites offering information about the hobby. As with any topic, researching aquarium information will turn up a lot of bad, misleading, or just plain wrong advice. As with any research project, when checking out aquarium-related material, you should check out your sources—check their credentials and experience, and cross-check the information against other sources. Remember, when dealing with living organisms, there are very few absolutes. One person's success or failure does not generalize to everyone else. And, of course, individual fish can appear or behave very differently from each other. People often need to be reminded that fish do not read books, but sometimes it seems as if they do read the books—and then take perverse delight in misbehaving!

Keep in mind that I have intentionally left out many subjects entirely to keep this book simple. Once you are an established aquarist, you can begin to explore any of those areas that interest you.

Enjoy your fish!

RESOURCES

Magazine

Tropical Fish Hobbyist
1 TFH Plaza
3rd & Union Avenues
Neptune City, NJ 07753
E-mail: info@tfh.com
www.tfhmagazine.com

Internet Resources

Aquaria Central
www.aquariacentral.com

Aquarium Hobbyist
www.aquariumhobbyist.com

C.A.R.E.S. Preservation
www.carespreservation.com

Cichlid Forum
www.cichlid-forum.com

Cichlids.com
www.cichlids.com

FishBase
www.fishbase.org

Loaches Online
www.loaches.com

Micrososm Aquarium Explorer
www.microsmaquarium
explorer.com

Planet Catfish
www.planetcatfish.com

TFH Magazine Forum (formerly Tropical Resources)
http://forums.tfhmagazine.com

WaterWolves
http://forums.waterwolves.com

Wet Web Media
www.wetwebmedia.com

A World of Fish
www.aworldoffish.com

Associations

American Cichlid Association
www.cichlid.org

American Killifish Association
www.aka.org

American Livebearer Association
http://livebearers.org

Books

Axelrod, Glen S. and Brian M. Scott. *The Encyclopedia of Exotic Tropical Fishes for Freshwater Aquariums.* TFH Publications, Inc.

Barber, Terry Anne and Rhonda Wilson. *The Simple Guide to Planted Aquariums.* TFH Publications, Inc.

Boruchowitz, David E. *Aquarium Care of Bettas.* TFH Publications, Inc.

Boruchowitz, David E. *Aquarium Care of Goldfish.* TFH Publications, Inc.

Boruchowitz, David E. *Freshwater Aquarium Problem Solver.* TFH Publications, Inc.

Boruchowitz, David E. *Mini-Aquariums.* TFH Publications, Inc.

Boruchowitz, David E. *PocketProfessional™ Guide to Cichlids.* TFH Publications, Inc.

Coletti, Ted Dengler. *Aquarium Care of Livebearers.* TFH Publications, Inc.

Dickinson, Claudia. *Aquarium Care of Cichlids.* TFH Publications, Inc.

Hellweg, Michael R. *Culturing Live Foods.* TFH Publications, Inc.

Jepson, Lance. *The Super Simple Guide to Common Fish Diseases.* TFH Publications, Inc.

Macdonald, Mark and Martin Thoene, eds. *Loaches.* TFH Publications, Inc.

Monks, Neale, ed. *Brackish-Water Fishes.* TFH Publications, Inc.

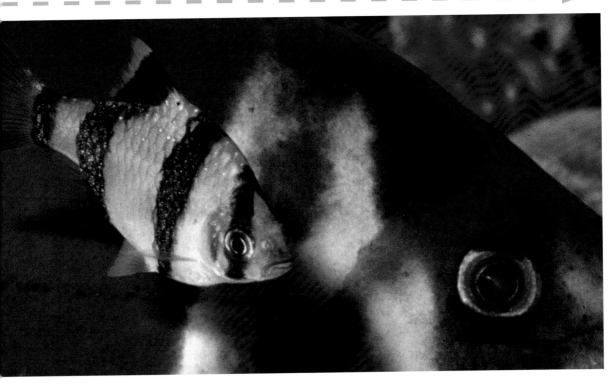

Muha, Laura. *The Super Simple Guide to Breeding Freshwater Fishes.* TFH Publications, Inc.

Pinkguni, Manolito. *The Guide to Owning Piranhas.* TFH Publications, Inc.

Pronek, Neal and Brian M. Scott. *Aquarium Care of Oscars.* TFH Publications, Inc.

Shubel, Stan. *Aquarium Care of Fancy Guppies.* TFH Publications, Inc.

Stansbury, Edward. *Breeding & Raising Angelfishes.* TFH Publications, Inc.

Sweeney, Mary E. *Adventurous Aquarist Guide™: The 101 Best Aquarium Plants.* Microcosm/TFH Publications, Inc.

Ward, Ashley. *Questions & Answers on Freshwater Aquarium Fishes.* TFH Publications, Inc.

Wood, Kathleen. *Adventurous Aquarist Guide™: The 101 Best Tropical Fishes.* Microcosm/TFH Publications, Inc.

Photo Credits

Page 16 Caption: The striking, patented red zebra danio is a relatively new arrival in the aquarium trade. Genetic engineering has produced *Danio rerio* in a variety of fluorescent colors, using genes from coral and jellyfish. The controversy surrounding other genetic engineering focuses on these fish as well, and in some places there are legal restrictions on them. Photo courtesy of Segrest Farms.

Jacqueline Abromeit (Shutterstock): 180

Joe Aliperti: 70

John Austin (Shutterstock): 45, 94

beltsazar (Shutterstock): 230

Dr. Warren E. Burgess: 190

Ken Childs: 42

Ted Dengler Coletti, Ph.D.: 131

Albert Connelly, Jr.: 55

Caleb Foster (Shutterstock): 148

Michael Gilroy: 26, 29, 127, 179, 189, 207, 209 (bottom-left)

Stefan Glebowski (Shutterstock): 96

Andreas Gradin (Shutterstock): 61, 72, 84

Harry Grier: 176

David Herlong: 112

Matthew Jacques (Shutterstock): 43

Jaroslav Kadlec: 205 (right)

Laila Kazakevica (Shutterstock): 117 (bottom)

Blaz Kure (Shutterstock): 102

Gary Lange: 74, 76, 83, 209 (bottom-right), 247, 251

Horst Linke: 91, 202, 224

Oliver Lucanus: 87, 165, 195, 200 (left), 213 (right), 243, 245

Jay Luto: 232, 249

Gary A. MacDonald: 21

Dmitrijs Mihejevs (Shutterstock): 20, 186

mypokcik (Shutterstock): 22

Aaron Norman: 10, 18, 32, 183, 211, 223 (right)

MP. & C. Piednoir: Front Cover, 7, 8, 19, 31, 47, 48, 49, 51, 62, 79, 107 (right), 147, 156, 161, 167 (top), 168, 192, 197, 198, 199 (left & right), 200 (right), 203 (left & right), 204 (left), 205 (left), 208, 213 (left), 219 (left & right), 223 (left), 227, 235, 239

Pieter (Shutterstock): 36

Andre Roth: 159, 184, 221 (left)

Marcelo Saavedra (Shutterstock): 4, 114, 119

salamanderman (Shutterstock): Back Cover, 34

Craig Sernotti: 67, 82, 100

Mark Smith: 14, 64, 167 (bottom), 201 (left)

Wolfgang Sommer: 132, 241

Ljupco Smokovski (Shutterstock): 253

Pawel Strykowski (Shutterstock): 73

Ed Taylor: 107 (left), 201 (right), 218, 237

Anthony C. Terceira: 81, 92, 135

Nikita Tiunov (Shutterstock): 233

Kostas Tsipos (Shutterstock): 138

Vilmos Varga (Shutterstock): 150

Rhonda Wilson: 137, 172

All other photos courtesy of the TFH Photo Archives

The World's Leading Aquarium Magazine
from the publishers of the world's finest aquarium books

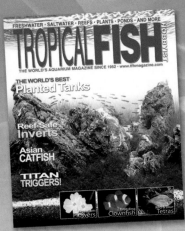

FRESHWATER • SALTWATER • REEFS • PLANTS • PONDS • AND MORE

FREE Gifts With Your Subscription:

• **FREE** *TFH* Aquatic Life Calendar • **FREE** Access to *TFH* Digital
• **FREE** book with 2-year subscription
Choose either *The 101 Best Saltwater Fishes* or *The 101 Best Tropical Fishes*
from the Microcosm/TFH Professional Series

Call for your **FREE** Trial Issue! 1-888-859-9034
www.tfhmagazine.com